Sacred Pilgrim, Secular Pilgrim:
A Roman Journey

Sacred Pilgrim, Secular Pilgrim

A Roman Journey

COLBY DICKINSON

CASCADE *Books* · Eugene, Oregon

SACRED PILGRIM, SECULAR PILGRIM
A Roman Journey

Copyright © 2025 Colby Dickinson. All rights reserved. Except for brief quotations in critical publications or reviews, no part of this book may be reproduced in any manner without prior written permission from the publisher. Write: Permissions, Wipf and Stock Publishers, 199 W. 8th Ave., Suite 3, Eugene, OR 97401.

Cascade Books
An Imprint of Wipf and Stock Publishers
199 W. 8th Ave., Suite 3
Eugene, OR 97401

www.wipfandstock.com

PAPERBACK ISBN: 979-8-3852-2104-2
HARDCOVER ISBN: 979-8-3852-2105-9
EBOOK ISBN: 979-8-3852-2106-6

Cataloguing-in-Publication data:

Names: Dickinson, Colby.

Title: Sacred pilgrim, secular pilgrim : a Roman journey / Colby Dickinson.

Description: Eugene, OR: Cascade Books, 2025 | Series: if applicable | Includes bibliographical references and index.

Identifiers: ISBN 979-8-3852-2104-2 (paperback) | ISBN 979-8-3852-2105-9 (hardcover) | ISBN 979-8-3852-2106-6 (ebook)

Subjects: LCSH: 1. Pilgrims and Pilgrimage. | 2. Rome—History. | 3. Memoir.

Classification: BV5067 D53 2025 (print) | BV5067 D53 (ebook)

Contents

Detailed Contents vii
Acknowledgments xv
Preface xvii

On the Aventine Hill 1
The Way of the Pilgrim 5
Rome 10
Along an Ancient Road 17
The Material Nature of Faith 26
Ongoing Distractions 34
Beyond Pilgrimage, Still a Pilgrim 40
Listening for Presence 45
The Layers of History 48
Life Suspended 54
Beyond the Walls 61
Fighting Modernity 68
Conversion of the Pilgrim 72
The Tensions of Purgatory 81
The Idol of Perfection 87
The Truth of Martyrdom 94
Grounding the Ungroundable 102
The Idol of Purity 110
Fabricating Yet Finding Sacrality 117
Epiphany 122
The Politics of Memory 126
Displays of Power 131
The Holy of Holies 141
Saint Peter's Basilica 145
Under the Dome 152

Contents

Contested Spaces 157
Tensions in the Body 165
Catechesis of the Relics 170
Consumerism 176
A Pilgrim's Church 179
Coda 189

Bibliography 197
Index 199

Detailed Contents

Chapter 1: On the Aventine Hill
The author comes to the top of the Aventine Hill, sitting in the orange garden—He feels skeptical, not trusting his own sentimentality—He wonders about his own mystical nature—He discovers his own sense of a sacrality that offers him a feeling of home

Chapter 2: The Way of the Pilgrim
He visits S. Silvestro in Capite, the head of John the Baptist—The basilica of S. Maria della Vittoria, Bernini's sculpture of Saint Teresa of Avila—He finds courage and indifference as two necessary characteristics of a pilgrim—Finding space for oneself amidst the bustling world—The path of the pilgrim as a waste of time—How a pilgrim achieves an intimacy that he can get from nothing else

Chapter 3: Rome
He describes the transformation of the pilgrim into the tourist—He moves to the catacombs of S. Callisto and S. Sebastiano, reminders of his own mortality—He accepts his life as he now finds it without any regret—He admits that only an openness to ambiguity can help him continuously learn to embrace

Chapter 4: Along an Ancient Road
He wanders along the Via Appia—He reflects on how life and death intersect and overlap—He reflects on the contrast between papal processions and the path of the pilgrim—He feels the loss of the original intent of pilgrimage

Detailed Contents

Chapter 5: The Material Nature of Faith
He finds tension between a loss of meaning and new experiences of modern art—He recognizes connections between art and spiritual insight—The tourist and the pilgrim as the same person—He feels the pilgrim's unwillingness to embrace poverty—He affirms that to know God is to know that one does not know much about God

Chapter 6: Ongoing Distraction
He enters S. Maria in Arcaelae and S. Lorenzo in Lucina—He witnesses the storm of modern consumerism among the tourists—He hopes the immeasurable value of silence in the midst of it all can be preserved—Keeping focus, resolve, and seriousness about the journey being made

Chapter 7: Beyond Pilgrimage, Still a Pilgrim
He visits S. Sabina on the Aventine Hill and wanders through the Testaccio area—He feels more at peace and uplifted when he is away from the "holy sites" and among the populace—The insight comes that no single modern phenomenon can replace religion; only a plurality of practices can form the religious dimensions of human existence—He visits the XII Apostles Church—He affirms the necessity for the pilgrim to encounter the twelve apostles—The uniqueness of Christianity not only in its religious, supernatural claims, but in its philosophical ones

Chapter 8: Listening for Presence
At the MACRO museum, he listens to experimental music—The only spiritual encounter with music that he has in Rome—He draws a parallel between his experiences and sitting in eucharistic adoration in Saint Louis, Missouri

Chapter 9: The Layers of History
Stemming the tide of religious decline by turning to the ground beneath the Church—Exploring underneath San Clemente—He finds a humbler version of Christian worship—S. Nicola Encarcere revealing Christianity's tendency to dominate historically over formerly pagan sites—To love the complexity of living in a world haunted by other presences

Detailed Contents

Chapter 10: Life Suspended

He recalls the destabilizing effects of his divorce—For him, the only path worthy for a pilgrim is the permanent interruption of life—He inhabits a secular perspective that nonetheless longs for a sacred encounter—He defines pilgrimage as a willingness to embrace a new life through a physical displacement that reflects the interior dislocation one already feels

Chapter 11: Beyond the Walls

He enters San Lorenzo fuori le mura—He recalls a personal triangulation: the end of his marriage, his broken foot, and a loss of faith—He feels disconnected from his former selves, yet also feels peace—He reflects on the tactics that Pope Pius IX used to save the Church from modernity and concludes that a future is possible—For him, both tradition and openness are needed for the Church's future—Knowing with certainty that his faith is gone, he finds himself more compelled than ever to go back inside the churches of Rome

Chapter 12: Fighting Modernity

He offers two examples of churches, Sacre Coeur basilica and Basilica del Sacro Cuore di Gesu, working to circumvent the rising currents of modern skepticism toward religious belief—He describes how Pope Pius X's pontificate tried to block the influences of modernity—He admits that such divisions are a distraction for the pilgrim—He also asks himself, as a pilgrim, how to transcend such divisions

Chapter 13: Conversion of the Pilgrim

He starts a new day at S. Agostino church and is drawn to Caravaggio's painting *Madonna of the Pilgrims*—He reflects upon the entanglement of Paul's conversion, bringing Judaic roots into his new life as a Christian—He, following Paul's lead, defines conversion as a change, a process of "turning around" that also entails a translation from one context to another—He visits San Paolo fuori le Mura and reflects upon the legend of Saint Paul's beheading—The modern pilgrim finds a richness in oneself by shutting off the distractions of modern society

Detailed Contents

Chapter 14: The Tensions of Purgatory
He reflects upon the Museum of Souls in Purgatory in the Sacred Heart of Jesus in Prati—He discusses the Catholic concept of purgatory and a tendency for a *both/and* logic in the Catholic faith—He expresses his own tensions between the faith of his childhood and the lack of his faith now—He also embraces the *both/and* principle, letting his tensions co-exist—He also ponders the Catholic question of religious pluralism

Chapter 15: The Idol of Perfection
He brings the Villa Medici as an ideal enclosed domestic space into conversation with idealized figures of the saints—He realizes that people aspire to ideals but never actually achieve them—Santa Maria degli Angeli as an example of the Catholic Church rebranding itself—Seeing a lack of divine intervention through the eyes of Galileo—For him, to be open to truth is to be open to one's own errors and vulnerabilities

Chapter 16: The Truth of Martyrdom
He reflects on the martyrdoms near the Pasquino statue in Piazza Navona—He goes on to describe the history of martyrdom in the early church—For him, the martyrs are the ones who ground themselves in their faith through an absurd choice—On the one hand, the martyr is an inspiration for the pilgrim who makes a foolish decision to waste their time and effort from the first moment of their journey—On the other hand, he also finds several differences between the martyr and the pilgrim

Chapter 17: Grounding the Ungroundable
He views and reflects upon the murals of martyrdom at Santo Stefano Rotondo and the church of S. Agnese in Agone—For him, faith is a relationship that attempts to ground the ungroundable—He also admits that faith is an interpersonal thing in which family and community are its center—Viewing the murals of the martyrs, he feels that faith is presented through art as clearly as if seen through relics

Chapter 18: The Idol of Purity
He focuses on Saints Agnese and Cecilia who are idealized in their martyrdoms for upholding faith—The potential misleading idealizations of purity

and holiness in young, female, virgin martyrs—He adds that martyrdom was the means to give a voice to the voiceless against their oppressors

Chapter 19: Fabricating Yet Finding Sacrality
He focuses on the Church of Santa Prassede where many dubious relics are located—Among these relics are those of Saints Valentine and Zeno, Prassede and Pudentiana—The pillar associated with Christ's death—He describes how ahistorical stories of saints go hand in hand with the creation of churches and the practice of faith

Chapter 20: Epiphany
He affirms that the pilgrim may be struck by an epiphany while listening for what comes from beyond the ordinary—He shows how revelation appears only with one's openness and receptivity—He recalls previous visits to St. Stephen's Cathedral in Vienna, the Cathedral Church of St. Peter in Cologne, and St. Bavo's Cathedral in Ghent—These churches, he reflects, seemed to unlock something within him that he had previously been unaware of—He concludes that only when one is able to accept the darkness within, can they accept the darkness of humanity

Chapter 21: The Politics of Memory
He mentions the history of Santa Maria in Trastevere—The politics of memory—What is preserved and what is repressed—He notices the juxtaposition of Mary as bearer of God and the rehabilitated image of a kidnapper and rapist Roberto Altemps—He explains that this juxtaposition is a sign of the tensions caused by the fusion of the spiritual and the material—The difficulty and biases of historical memory

Chapter 22: Displays of Power
He reflects on San Giovanni in Laterano, Rome's first true Christian basilica—A historical site of the papal residences—He explains the overlap of the spiritual and the political in the basilica—For him, a great deal is possible in terms of reaching the "highest heights" and "lowest lows" within such sacred spaces

DETAILED CONTENTS

Chapter 23: The Holy of Holies
He realizes that his own life at the moment reflects both absences and longings, he wanders looking for the feeling of being at home—He further focuses on the Lateran—He explains how the Church unknowingly created museum spaces as secularized versions of sacred places—How material, previously housed at the Lateran, was moved to the Vatican museums—He emphasizes the thin line between the museum and sacred spaces

Chapter 24: Saint Peter's Basilica
He recalls the first time he visited Saint Peter's square on his honeymoon years ago, longing for transcendence and connection in his marriage—He focuses on the figure of Peter as a figure of tensions—He feels the tension between belief and unbelief in his inner soul—He finds the mystery of faith through allowing the materiality of life to overwhelm and overtake the spirituality of his self—He realizes that his loss of belief is inseparable from his faith—He believes that only by allowing the dark interior to engulf and enrich him with its force, can he enter the brightness of the light

Chapter 25: Under the Dome
He briefly describes different popes' attitudes toward Vatican II—He affirms that even in a space of political power, there are moments that seem to transcend the ordinary run of things—For him, San Pietro may be the last place one can make an emotionally meaningful pilgrimage—He believes that pilgrimage is the journey of walking through this world awakened to life in whatever space we might truly find and embrace it

Chapter 26: Contested Spaces
He presents two contested spaces: Santa Maria sopra Minerva, built over a Roman temple to Isis, and as a burial site to many popes, and the Pantheon, a pagan site and the burial site of the first king of Italy—He explains that Santa Maria sopra Minerva represents the collusion of different religious traditions and divergent views within the Catholic Church itself—The Pantheon, according to him, shows the plurality of our world today and its syncretistic desires—He points out that these contested spaces reflect the politics of personal faith today

Detailed Contents

Chapter 27: Tensions in the Body
He visits a small church named after Ss. Giovanni e Paulo—He is reminded of the many tensions that the Catholic Church embodies—He is drawn to these tensions and does not wish to dispel them—He finds these tensions expand his vision in multiple historical directions at once—He also finds that these irresolvable tensions serve to further heighten other pressures regarding the dimensions of sacrality in our world

Chapter 28: Catechesis of the Relics
He comes to Santa Croce in Gerusalemme—He distinguishes between the solitude that helps to recapture the essence of pilgrimage and modern forms of isolation—He discovers that this chapel of relics draws the pilgrim inward—For him, Santa Croce is not just a symbol of faith, but the faith itself—He respects those who come to the chapel of relics to find a union of the spiritual and the material, a union that comprises life—He also welcomes disruptions and his openness provides renewal

Chapter 29: Consumerism
He reflects upon the major retail center on Via del Corso, running straight from the Piazza del Popolo, where Goethe once lived—He compares his objections against the invasion of capitalism to Luther's protestations against the corruptions that plagued Rome in the sixteenth century—For him, this consumerism within Rome gives rise to reflections on pilgrimage and a desire to commune with the past

Chapter 30: A Pilgrim's Church
He focuses on the basilica of Santa Maria Maggiore—He presents a convergence of many aspects of church history—Colonization, papal authority, pilgrimage, and the history of Marian devotion all appear on this sacred site—How learning to be a pilgrim means learning to construct an internal order that gently shelters—Building a chamber of solitude, not to reject the world but to find stability and solace in its midst

Acknowledgments

I OWE A MAJOR debt of gratitude to the faculty and staff at Loyola University Chicago's John Felice Rome Center, which often hosted me during my many stays in Rome. I am grateful especially to Mark Bosco for inviting me to the opportunity to teach a course on pilgrimage in Rome and to Stefano Giacchetti whose wonderfully organized conferences on Critical Theory drew me to Rome as much as the history, art, and architecture. Conversations there with Hille Haker, David Ingram, Andrew Cutrofello, and Hugh Miller always spurred more thought than I could handle.

A research grant from Loyola University Chicago enabled me to focus on this project at a time when I deeply needed to, and for that a big thanks must also be extended to the university administration who make such research possible.

I wish to express my thanks to many people in my department who have aided me in ways both direct and indirect as I worked toward completing this project. Some journeyed to Rome and accompanied me there in different ways, some were stable presences in Chicago who helped foster an atmosphere conducive to the work I was doing. My gratitude for them all is abundant. I thank especially Aana Vigen, Mara Brecht, Mark Bosco, Bret Lewis, Hugh Nicholson, Lauren O'Connell, Xueying Wang, Josefrayn Sánchez-Perry, Chris Skinner, Bob DiVito, Joanne Brandstrader, Hille Haker, Miguel Díaz, and Randy Newman.

There were numerous conversations while in Rome that stimulated my research and kept me company along the way, especially those with Gábor Ambrus, Cristina Lombardi, Kristien Justaert, Tom Jacobs, Marcos Norris, Ron and Phyllis Dickinson, Rowan Bayley, and Elisabeth Bayley.

A special thanks to Katie Marshall for buoying my spirits with the classic film *Roman Holiday* while I was unable to travel there during the pandemic.

Acknowledgments

Many thanks are extended as well to Jack Nuelle and Whitney Harper for their help with getting this text into shape prior to its publication, as well as Sr. Su Pham for drafting the short summaries at the beginning of each chapter.

Preface

A CONVERSATION IN ROME recently reminded me how important writing this book on pilgrimage was to me. I had been saying something to my friend Gábor about how I had written so many books already, but rarely did any one of them speak to me as if the words had come out of my own mouth, as if they resonated with the deepest recesses of my own soul. There was a part of me that was left behind, that was somehow not included in the conversation.

He responded to my frustration at not yet finding my voice as a writer by correcting me: "Academic writers don't have a voice. That's not their concern. You want something different, something better." He correctly pointed out that I wanted a form of integrity as a writer that so many academic voices could not embody.

All too often in academic prose, there is mostly description, argument, judgment, or conclusion, rather than the poetry and the beauty of writing, praise for ambiguity, recognition of the complexity of life, and of our failure to depict such a reality with words. To be fair, these are more literary than academic affairs, though I long to find some way to bring these disparate worlds into a harmonious orbit with one another.

What would it mean for a writer to be a pilgrim through language, meandering over the challenges and personal encounters made along the way, rather than to write with an aim toward mastery and understanding?

Finding one's voice and then letting that voice lead you as a writer should be an experience that is recognized and embraced by those around us as much as by the one who has the experience. It is the creation and use of a fearless speech that may, however, trouble some who may not want to hear what another has to say.

Preface

I can understand how, for so many people, it feels impossible to locate this fearless speech within themselves because they have not felt supported or loved in their personal, intimate life. Too many forget that love means being willing to let go of the one you love and to allow them the freedom to be themselves at all costs.

I think of these things when I pause to consider how leaving religious faith and community behind have been crucial for me in finding my voice as a writer and as a human being. I needed, and continue to need, to speak without the fear of rejection or judgment lurking in my mind's eye, and leaving behind a community of faith allowed me to find that freedom—even if I return someday.

At the same time, I also realize why it had taken so long for me to do this, as, for years, I had struggled to feel accepted within the most intimate spheres of my home life as well. It is very difficult to stand confident in one's own space, to hear one's own voice rising, without a foundation underneath one's own feet. Our social identities and the structures that maintain them—such as with religion, one's career, marriage, and so forth—are meant to ease the burdens of our construction of ourselves. But sometimes they are additional burdens that hamper us from connecting with others and with ourselves.

When these social identities collapse, we begin a journey into the abyss of meaning, where it feels as if all senses of the self, and the purpose and meaning that accompanied us, has been dissolved. This experience of depletion, and the exhaustion that follows, can be a terribly precarious place to find one's way out of. At the same time, the tangled forces of each social identity, as they converge in the singular selves we always are, can become knotted together, impossible to disentangle and needing to be separated and pressed smooth so that some may be retained and some discarded, or reinvented altogether.

When these forces coalesced at a particular point in my life, and the mess became too much to bear, I felt that I had to find new paths to walk down where none had previously existed. I felt it was time to embrace the life of the pilgrim.

I brought together my many travels to Rome on pilgrimage and the extremely diverse spiritual experiences that I had had while there and began to collate my thoughts, feelings, and notes in order to write the book that lays before you. It was time to pull myself together and to suture the

Preface

vulnerabilities that had prevented me from feeling closure and clarity for so long.

For the main two years of the pandemic, I could not finish this book. Some suggested that I make a concerted effort during an awkwardly scheduled sabbatical to write about Roman pilgrimage, but I could not. My son had just started high school and I felt I needed to remain close to home.

Above all, I was unable to fly to Rome. So, instead, I simply organized my notes, read up on the city, its past and present, and waited until I could return there in person to experience it once again as the odd pilgrim that I am.

As soon as I was finally able to return, I unlocked something inside myself, and the words poured forth. I wrote prolifically in a notebook while stopped at cafes, along sidewalks, and on church steps under the hot Roman sun. I wrote sitting under magnificent domes and in quiet gardens, on park benches and against walls while standing and avoiding the hordes of tourists.

Nearly every moment, I found, was one for reflecting and, so too, for writing.

For the medieval pilgrim there were guides such as The *Mirabilia Urbis Romae*, or "The Wonders of the City of Rome," a compendium of miraculous sites around the city that guided pilgrims through town.[1] Today there are secular, historical guides to educate tourists eager to know more about what it is that they are experiencing in this beautiful city. I knew, however, that what I was writing was neither a pilgrim's nor a tourist's guide to Rome, though both types of writings were my companions from time to time.[2]

Pilgrimage, as André Brouillette has aptly described it, is a plurality of experiences, involving complex interactions between one's intentions, moments of transcendence, resonances of personal and historical memory, vulnerabilities and a willingness to undergo transformation, immersion into foreignness and otherness, devotional practices and beliefs, the specific nature of the places one journeys to, and how one's very body comports them there and allows them to experience the extraordinary.[3] It is only through the

---

1. Addis, *Eternal City*, 296–300.
2. For example, I think here of Rear, *Rome*; Schmisek, *Rome of Peter and Paul*; Erasmo, *Strolling Through Rome*; and Heath, *Architecture Lover's Guide to Rome*.
3. Brouillette, *Pilgrim Paradigm*, 13–45.

Preface

unique combination of these extremely complex factors and idiosyncratic, personal elements that one can come to experience pilgrimage as an entirely singular event in one's life.

Any definition of pilgrimage, moreover, will always be provisional and enveloped by a series of embodied rituals and practices, all dependent upon the religions and traditions that govern them to some degree.[4]

Pilgrimage is at times little more than a search for peace amidst the always personal challenge to locate a meaningful relationship to the question of God.[5]

In a simplistic but straightforward way, I like to imagine that a pilgrimage takes place for me whenever I allow myself to be attentive to a specific geographical place and so to experience, mind, body, and soul, a deep resonance with forces larger than myself, whatever those may be.[6] I listen in ways that I normally do not, and I am transformed by measures I cannot expect.

I consider my personal faith life as a pilgrimage, and not simply a theoretical exercise.

I move from one position to another in search of depth, integrity, and encounter, not sure of where I am going or where I will end up, but intentionally searching for meaning and purpose with every step, hopeful that if undergone with a spirit of humility and awareness, I might just access a profound and unexpected presence.

For many, such a faith journey may itself appear to contain too much uncertainty, too great a mystery, and too few answers. But, for the pilgrim, this journey cannot be taken in any other way. It is my openness to the life that awaits me on the paths I walk down that brings about new forms of encounter, and eventual relationship, with those before me.

It is important to state that I did not follow a specific pilgrimage route in Rome, and I do not follow one in what I ended up recording in these pages. I intentionally broke with tradition to a large degree, as well as those inscribed rituals to be found in Catholic practices. While I honored their core, I also rewrote them entirely, making them personal and my own.

---

4. Coleman, *Powers of Pilgrimage*.

5. See the accounts of pilgrimage as a struggle with faith given in Mahoney, *Singular Pilgrim*, and Egan, *Pilgrimage to Eternity*.

6. See the account of resonant experiences given in Rosa, *Resonance*.

Preface

It is likewise important to recognize, to myself, that I felt no obligation to take a pilgrimage, and that this absence of obligation is precisely what allowed me, in the end, to be a pilgrim. I find that, by engaging the practice of pilgrimage, there is no other way to connect to myself, to confront myself, and to confess myself than by merging the physical-geographical-material nature of my existence with the theoretical-spiritual side of who I am and who I will always be.

Pilgrimage is where my theoretical concepts are interwoven with my embodied life in helpful ways—in life-giving ways. I must honor them as such or they simply will not intertwine, and should be abandoned or rethought.

Whatever this thing called soul is within me, it can only become manifest by placing it in ceaseless dialogue with everything around me—the places, people, and presences that I immerse myself in, that I am present to and cultivate as sources of resonance with my life. I crave a resonance with the world around me, as Hartmut Rosa has put it, because I become uniquely alive in such moments, where what I cannot control becomes more steadily the thing I am oriented toward.[7]

It is in this sense that I departed from religious tradition in order to rediscover something like the core of what it means to be religious at all. Hence, I left my Catholicism behind even as I entered through its doors and knelt on its grounds.

I suspended all judgment in order to learn a more proper internal judgment.

I found sacred spaces potentially anywhere because there is a sacred space deep within me that I cannot ignore and that guided me to each place in the city, if I only listened well enough and followed.

There is a sparsity to my thoughts when I walk, as if all extraneous thought were absent for its duration. This was the spirit with which I undertook writing about pilgrimage in this book.

When I finally stop to record my thoughts, the brevity and density of my words reflect this state of embodied focus. I have little use for ornamentation in such spaces, though there are those occasional sublime moments when beauty cuts through the clouds and fixes its radiance upon me. Gratitude inevitably follows.

---

7. Rosa, *Resonance*.

Preface

When I was a child, there was a daily inclination toward acceptance of the solitary pursuits that drew me: whatever gave wonder, pleasure, challenge, and excitement was that which I immersed myself in that much further. I delighted too in my social life and in play with others. A balance was essential and I would rush to and from each endeavor. Having the stability of a playmate as a child, such as my brother and the friends I then had, was essential, as too much alone time wasn't desirable and could even provoke a childish despair that there was no one to play with, no one to watch me, no one to notice what I was doing.

The major struggle I face now, at this stage in my adult life, is the same in some ways: constant interaction when I want it and rushing excitedly to my solitary work and writing when I want that too. Yet, I have little patience for the balance I seek, nor any reliance on another person that is constant and foundational, and I despair at times in the most childish fashion.

It is good to be alone at times, immersed in solitude, and to feel deeply within me a longing for connection. It is good and proper not to run anxiously toward a relationship in order to escape having to face my fears of solitude. Though to merely sit in this space can also all too quickly become an act of desperation that exhausts itself in the shallowness of encounters that do not speak to the depths of my soul. It is like eating a fine dessert in front of the television and failing to notice the taste of what you are eating.

Solitude, the solitary state of the pilgrim, refocuses us on what matters most. Paradoxically, by being alone, we can appreciate the meaning and joy of relationship and the presence of love in our lives.

This is not to say that I enjoy being alone. In fact, mostly I do not. It is rather that I need to make the space available to myself so that I might be more present to others when I am with them. Allowing myself to be terrorized by my solitariness, for example, only defeats the possibility of experiencing greater depths of intimacy when I am with others. I know this to be true even though I struggle with the reality of my aloneness most days. This is why I needed—and still very much need—to go on these spiritual journeys by myself in order to locate and make peace with this debilitating madness inside me.

Sitting in the airport on my way back to Rome after the pandemic, feeling the weight of the solitary journey upon me, I wondered what would be different this time from all of the other times I had visited Rome, where the loneliness of everyday life often propelled me on paths of desperation and hasty decisions.

I don't know if these reflections are how a pilgrimage should begin, mired in doubt and speculation rather than meditatively centering myself on the voice, or voices, within me. It felt like the wrong way to begin such a journey, as I was not focused on the necessity of an inner transformation, the desire for it, the integrating force that centering one's self can bring. Looking back, I also wondered if I needed to be in any particular frame of mind for the pilgrimage to be effective.

An essential part of the pilgrimage, perhaps the most consequential portion, is allowing yourself to encounter whatever it is that you encounter, whatever it is that you hear speaking to you at whatever point you receive insight or illumination.

Traditionally, there are many theological modes of existence where one simply waits to receive an unmerited gift—a particular grace—that comes unexpectedly and without one's having earned it. Is this not how life sometimes acts upon us?

Is it a form of magical thinking to hope for such an unearned transformation? Is it wrong to long with every fiber of your being for the presence of another to reach out and touch you? What is this endless craving for love, forgiveness, or companionship for if it will never find fulfillment in one's lived, everyday life?

Maybe I am being shaped by this longing right now in ways unobserved that will yet form me profoundly in the direction I need to go, in ways most essential to my nature and vocation, even without a god to predestine that it must unfold in some particular way.

Maybe I am being deepened by this secular fate to become who I must become.

There are many, no doubt, who live and die with unfulfilled dreams, who meet a tragic end without having obtained any lasting sense of what it would have been like to locate something like fulfillment of their deepest hopes and wishes within this short life.

I feel selfish and entitled to even contemplate a different ending to my own brief run on this planet. Yet no amount of meditation on the fleetingness and contingency of human happiness can dissuade me from the desire to wander aimlessly but directly so as to experience a feeling of being at home in my own life in a way that I have never yet known.

Pilgrimage is a sort of willingness to accept one's exile from the routines of daily life, but it is not the cure for an existential homelessness. It does not magically repair the broken dreams that push me onto the pilgrim's path, and yet it feels central to the processes of locating them nonetheless.

I do not want to live the rest of my life waiting for happiness to happen and never experience the fullness it can bring. I want to live by cultivating the happiness that is in my life now, as it exists, in whatever form it takes, even when, and especially when, I don't recognize my life as either happy or peaceful.

Somehow, without even knowing fully how, pilgrimage offers a way toward this aim.

Allowing myself to be overcome by the experience of being a pilgrim who is open to those unknown twists and turns that confront them is an exercise in learning to wander toward a deeper sense of fulfilment, one that all too often eludes me.

It dawns on me that rather than be the passive victim of hopelessness, perhaps it is that I have not truly let myself hope. I have stopped myself from daring to hope because, as is the case for many of us, I have been so afraid of being disappointed.

But what if I hoped and allowed myself to dwell lastingly in such hope; to imagine the happiness and fulfillment that awaits me in another future, that follows me to a beautiful place and to the home I have always imagined? Or what if I abandoned all hope, allowing new paths to open up beyond the illusions and stagnant desire that hope at times fosters?

It strikes me that this would be to let myself believe, to have faith and to be moored by it. But I am kept at a distance from such a faith at the same as I court it.

I want to list my hopes and dreams again. I want to live by them, honoring them, to confide my secret dreams to myself and to live with them beside me at all times as a welcomed presence.

I took these things with me on my pilgrimage, unresolved, swallowed at times whole by despair and desperation, and at other times appearing over the horizon just a step or two ahead of me. At other times, they surfaced from within me, even if just for a moment, and guided me along my path.

Preface

A pilgrimage traditionally conceived starts from one's home and heads in a particular direction toward a specific destination. The medieval pilgrimage to Rome or Jerusalem, for example, reflected the Christian's desire to ascend to heaven, the long sought after kingdom of God.

To this day, pilgrims routinely make journeys, whether to Lourdes, Fatima, Guadalupe, Santiago de Compostella, Assisi, Jerusalem, or Rome, in order to locate something for which they have been searching: healing, perhaps, or grace; forgiveness or personal insight. But such things do not just come from these specific, earthly locales. They come too from living one's life *as* a pilgrim, especially when there is no set destination for one's journey.

The pilgrimage through Rome I record in these pages had no set destination other than Rome itself. What every pilgrim finds at some point is that, even upon arriving at one's destination, there is still a meandering about the place that unravels one's focus, a moment of recognition that one can be just as lost *after* arriving as they were on the trail to arrive there, or before they had even set out.

Our anticipation and longing meet frustration when we realize that the destination we have arrived at contains perhaps no more revelation than what we might find within our own homes. The external search may be no different from the internal, and our entire journey not worth the time we had spent in taking it.

John Bunyan's *The Pilgrim's Progress* introduced a Protestant critique of Catholic pilgrimage to the Christian world, wherein it was demonstrated that one can make the journey toward God without leaving one's home. There was no need for pilgrimage to involve pageantry, indulgences, or the physically taxing journey itself insofar as one could undertake a trip to divine insight through a purely internal, spiritual framework.

Bunyan was in many ways right, of course, though, in its own way, so is the Catholic tradition of physically undertaking a pilgrimage to a specific sacred site. Both contain elements of truth about how our rational and embodied selves must comport themselves in this world in order to encounter that thing still deeper within us called spirit or soul.

The truth can be discerned through the tension these positions create for us: we do not have to aim for a specific location or end result in order to live the truth of the pilgrim. But we are also aided in significant ways through embodying the journey and not just reducing it to its abstract,

Preface

spiritual elements. We are, after all, fit with bodies that move through space and time, and in need of knowing what they say to us, how they are in fact inextricably intertwined with us.

Pilgrimage is, then, a way of living, not just a journey with a fixed end point. It is a wandering without end that nonetheless brings us before moments of transcendent insight, revelation, and ecstatic joy while also acquainting us more intimately with our limitations, our failures, and our deepest fears.

Pilgrimage is an attitude that brings us humbly to kneel before that which is much larger than ourselves, just as it opens us up to ourselves at our deepest points at the same time.

What follows are my notes from various pilgrimages to Rome, often recorded as they were written while I was there, even if these meditations reflect different periods of time in my life and different experiences undergone while there. My desire was to immerse the reader in the heat of the experience and so to forego a chronological narrative, even as autobiographical fragments do appear in the margins from time to time. I invite the reader to put their own life in dialogue with their journey and to examine themselves as the pilgrim that they too always are.

On the Aventine Hill

The author comes to the top of the Aventine Hill—Sitting in the orange garden—He feels skeptical, not trusting his own sentimentality—He wonders about his own mystical nature—He discovers his own sense of a sacrality that offers him a feeling of home

IT DOES NOT BOTHER me in the slightest—in fact it feels *true* in a deep, internally resonant way—that, despite my not having faith in God, I continue to feel drawn, time and again, to sites of the sacred and the holy. These places set apart from the ordinary run of life are a continual sign to me that I am repeatedly called to interrupt my life, my own humanity even, in order to recognize that which is and will forever be beyond me and my understanding. I am called by life itself, as it were, to recognize that there are points in life's journey where signs themselves will no longer be given or received, and that, despite this lack, indeed because I can feel this lack acutely, I am a pilgrim searching for something I cannot possess.

I believe this comprehension of an ambiguity I will never resolve is why I like to sit in the orange garden just to the side of Santa Sabina along the top of the Aventine Hill in Rome as often as I can. As I stare out over the hilltop to the flowing waters of the Tiber below, I feel a sufficient closeness, but also a distance from the organized life of the Catholic Church. It is not my religion anymore, but it is a shelter and a destination, and even, in ways I am still trying to grasp, a home.

It is not the lack of art or mosaics inside this particular church, which once used to dazzle the eyes of pilgrims who had made long, arduous journeys to Rome over mountains and rivers, that keeps me at a certain remove. It is something else that lingers along with the scents of the garden.

Sacred Pilgrim, Secular Pilgrim

I am well aware of the powerful conversionary experience once undergone by the American Trappist monk Thomas Merton inside this particular church, where Saint Thomas Aquinas himself had resided in the thirteenth century. But I feel caught, happily, between Merton's openness, displayed through his youthful embrace of faith, and his later critique of his own interpretations of the event, how he himself came to question the rose-colored hues that he had once attached to his religious zeal.[1]

Being old enough now, perhaps even wise enough, to not trust my own sentimentality, which leaves me both skeptical and more open to newness than I have ever been in my life, there is an ease within me that wells up when sitting so close to something with which I am also so distant.

Somehow residing in paradox while being considerate of the beauty and the impact made upon me, I am able to overlook the city, with its late afternoon sepia tint of rooftops and domes, finding a place within myself that speaks louder than any other sound.

Isn't that what, for centuries, the mystics really listened to in their own way?

I continue to wonder about my own mystical nature while allowing for voices from the past to speak to me about their own experiences as well. That is what I find here and in each of the many churches of Rome: the onslaught of voices telling me about their experience of the sacred, not abstractly, but in this particular place, at a particular moment in time.

I find I cannot look away and I cannot escape from the lessons they leave with me.

༄

The walls of the garden just behind me secure the panorama resting before my sight, allowing me to feel secure and without any shame at being wholly beyond whatever claims I had once thought held me fast in matters of faith. It is as if I, an ambiguous combination of body and soul, am loosed upon the horizon, able to soar out over it, aware of what I am leaving behind me on the ground below, while also reaching out to whatever lies even further out beyond me, what I will never be able to grasp entirely, if at all.

I do not know if the peace or upheaval that mystics and saints have felt inside themselves throughout the centuries are the same feelings I get when

---

1. Merton, *Seven Storey Mountain*, 113.

I look at the city from this vantage point, but a similar resonance must at least be partially present within us all when faced with similar encounters.

I am reminded of how much Saint Augustine once struggled to define his God, and how much I enjoy his failures and successes in doing so: "there is a light I love, and a food, and a kind of embrace when I love my God—a light, voice, odour, food, embrace of my inner man, where my soul is flood-lit by light which space cannot contain, where there is sound that time cannot seize, where there is a perfume which no breeze disperses, where there is a taste for food no amount of eating can lessen, and where there is a bond of union that no satiety can part. That is what I love when I love my God".[2]

Sitting in the park until dusk, listening to a street musician forage from each passerby, and slowly turning my back, never fully, to the nondescript brick façade of one of the earliest churches in Rome, I am carried onto the sidewalks and backstreets of a warm night, the smell of the orange trees lingering with me well after it should have departed.

What I hear echoing within me at the moment I descend from the Aventine Hill I am able to place my finger on later that night when reading a French philosopher against the slope of a rooftop terrace:

> Divine places, without gods, with no god, are spread out everywhere around us, open and offered to our coming, to our going or to our presence, give up or promised to our visitation, to frequentation by those who are not men either, but who are there, in these places: ourselves, alone, out to meet that which we are not, and which the gods for their part have never been. These places, spread out everywhere, yield up and orient new spaces: they are no longer temples, but rather the opening up and the spacing out of the temples themselves, a dis-location with no reserve henceforth, with no more sacred enclosures—other tracks, other ways, other places for all who are there.[3]

I am no longer held so tightly, enclosed and comforted by religion, but I dwell in these spaces between what had once held me closely. Now, at long last on this journey of my life, I am ready to encounter that which

---

2. Augustine, *Confessions*, 183.
3. Nancy, *Inoperative Community*, 150.

I am not, and to remake myself along the way as the wayward pilgrim that I have become.

I own the notion of the pilgrim, readapted from its religious roots and displaced onto the life that I now lead. If being dislocated from one's life is a true hallmark of conversion, I hope there is something of the sacred yet *beyond the traditionally sacred* within my journey as well, though I have no doubt it will look nothing like the sacred as humanity has often crafted it to be.

There is no sense of a sacrality that binds me, encloses itself upon me, as it has done throughout history to so many. But there is a sense of the sacred here nonetheless, one that reaches out to me and offers me a feeling of home while letting me know that home is not what I had previously imagined it to be.

I walk on throughout the night, following odd, narrow streets down whatever course they run. I benefit from neither knowing nor searching for a destination.

The Way of the Pilgrim

He visits S. Silvestro in Capite, the head of John the Baptist—The basilica of S. Maria della Vittoria, Bernini's sculpture of Saint Teresa of Avila—He finds courage and indifference as two necessary characteristics of a pilgrim—Finding space for oneself amidst the bustling world—The path of the pilgrim as a waste of time—How a pilgrim achieves an intimacy that he can get from nothing else

To be a pilgrim is to recognize a union of body and spirit, one made manifest by the rhythms of hunger, walking, thirst, solitude, and a desire for what lies beyond, *always beyond*. What we are surrounded by every day is not necessarily what we are seeking after with our deepest longings and our fractured desires. At times, the pilgrim is reminded, we need to remove ourselves from the routines of our daily lives in order to engage more deeply with what transcends us, and so, in turn, to see ourselves anew.

To be immersed in the immediacies of life is to be submerged in the domestic patterns and social economies that inherently limit our capacity for self-awareness. A pilgrim is the one who knows they must step away from all of this in order to see something that cannot ordinarily be seen by human eyes.

I feel this distinction the moment I step into broad daylight upon the streets of Rome and begin to walk with or without a destination in mind, letting myself drift through beautiful spaces intended for meditation so that I might witness my life as an outsider to it.

꙳

I know I am not the typical pilgrim, but my acceptance of my fear in facing the unknown—which can never be completely removed, but only recognized and accepted—I feel, is enough to qualify me as one. So I defend the identity of the pilgrim and the art of pilgrimage, hoping they never fade from human existence and that I might somehow invest myself further in their mysteries. Their significance is of the utmost importance, especially now in the secular age in which we live.

I think of these things when visiting S. Silvestro in Capite, a church which claims to have the head of John the Baptist in a small side chapel. Mass at noon had about a total of three people in attendance, plus a homeless man sitting outside in the courtyard. Five tourists departed from its sanctuary the moment mass began.

I thought something similar too when visiting the basilica of S. Maria della Vittoria where a smattering of people had come to see Bernini's sculpture of Saint Teresa of Ávila in her orgasmic pose of being struck by divine love. No one genuflected, nor did anyone hesitate to snap a quick photo of this masterpiece of form.

An elderly monk sat in his cowl just behind the altar railing, watching the scene unfold without the slightest expression on his face. So much colored marble and gold packed into this tight space, everything elegantly decorated as a fitting repository for Bernini's work, but not, most hours, a space for either liturgy or prayer.

෴

There are many routes already taken daily upon which we do not reflect: the workers making their daily deliveries, the families on their way to school and the office, the hordes of tourists charting a course to museums or parks, even those religious individuals on a path to one of the city's many churches.

It is possible, even likely, that the religious person may be making the journey to an ostensibly sacred place without the pilgrim's intent guiding them toward their destination. The route of the pilgrim will overlap with some of these other routes, but will also subvert them, perhaps ignore them. The pilgrim is indifferent to them, and this gesture of indifference is what sets them apart, what risks incurring the anger of others, or at least their frustration.

It is also what provides the pilgrim with a hidden, inner wisdom that radiates far beyond their personal life.

Wisdom can only be achieved by subverting the everyday logics of the world, by removing oneself from the ordinary in order to see what others do not see, what they may, in fact, refuse to see. The pilgrim searches endlessly for this wisdom especially and allows themselves to go against the grain of efficiency and productivity that our modern, capitalist world prizes, in order to grow and mature in spirit, which is to say, in secret or without the world taking notice.

To be a pilgrim is to seek out a space for oneself amidst the frenetic activity of the world in order to cultivate an interior space that others hardly know exists. This is generally why the pilgrim walks alone, or at least expects to walk alone, and does not care if they make the journey by themselves, even if others are present alongside them on the pilgrimage.

Every pilgrimage will be different for each pilgrim, depending on the context, opportunities, and limitations of one's life at a precise moment in time. Embracing the particularities of one's situation, even of one's body and embodied way of being in the world, are crucial to what is experienced and learnt along the way.

There is a courage and an indifference that follows the pilgrim down every path they take, and these traits must become the character of the pilgrim if they are to accrue into anything like wisdom.

Typically, I see few souls walking from the distant catacombs along the Via Appia to the central churches of Rome. I don't think I am special for being the only one I see walking such routes throughout the city, intent on finding a deeper meaning for my journey. But this physical solitude is already an indication that the nature of pilgrimage, especially in a city revered by so many as containing the presence of holiness, is lost to many—or perhaps not completely lost, just unknown and undiscovered.

*

Wisdom is a practice, taking time to accumulate and earn within one's lifetime. Wisdom is picked up along a journey, not given gratuitously all at once, as if descended straight from the heavens.

The pilgrim intuitively understands this to be true. The pilgrim accepts this reality and knows there is no other way by which to gain that understanding that so many want to gain but all too often lack the will to undertake. This is why the pilgrim is the one who merely places one foot in front of the other, who keeps going when so many others have given up. It is why the pilgrim regards the journey as just as important as the destination, because not one inch of the road can be forsaken or omitted.

The pilgrim accepts this state of affairs and, moreover, embraces it as their own rootless root. Therein lies the wisdom that becomes theirs once the process that is pilgrimage has been embraced.

&

If one were to suggest that the pilgrim indulges in wasting time through the circuitous routes they employ, one would be correct. The path of the pilgrim, like the penitent who is thoughtfully lost in prayer, is a master at wasting time. Prayer itself is a wasting of one's time. But this wasting, so counterproductive to the various economies of the world, is precisely the display of wisdom that the world misses.

Processes crucial to the formation of the self, even to the ambiguous form of the soul, take place in this act of wasting and are essential to wisdom's coming to be.

&

I have often noted how our only true friends, like those we still maintain from our childhood, are those we are most capable of wasting time with. The frivolity displayed toward time in our youth displays a willingness to meet one another in play, a suspension of the world's efficiencies and demands that otherwise dominate our outlooks on a "life well lived." What is gained in this wasting of time is a closeness, a proximity, an intimacy that nothing else can provide. This is what the pilgrim, ever the internal child, knows to be true and so claims as their own.

I long for such companions who likewise value this wasting of time. I long to immerse myself in such play as it generates deeper connections than can be seen or described.

&

The joys of wandering, of deep peregrination, of happy discovery, are all present to the pilgrim because they have detached themselves from the normal state of things and have allowed themselves to waste what is otherwise valued so heavily elsewhere.

The pilgrim recognizes that what is usually valued in this world has a weight that wears one down; a burden that must be shed if one is going to see the realities lying underneath it all. Spiritualities that give caution concerning the need to renounce worldly possessions and money abound for a reason.

The pilgrim is the one who intuitively knows these teachings to be true. Understanding this state of affairs brings about an inherent wisdom the pilgrim gains for themselves by simply following the path under their feet toward a holiness that seems to always lie beyond them.

Rome

He describes the transformation of the pilgrim into the tourist—He moves to the catacombs of S. Callisto and S. Sebastiano, reminders of his own mortality—He accepts his life as he now finds it without any regret—He admits that only an openness to ambiguity can help him continuously learn to embrace

THERE'S A PASSAGE ON Rome in the poet Rainer Maria Rilke's letters that strikes me as the reflection of one in pursuit of the same kind of wisdom that the pilgrim in Rome seeks. Reality's clash with solitude and the cultivated attentiveness to beauty of the pilgrim pour forth from every word he once wrote:

> We arrived in Rome about six weeks ago, at a time when it was still the empty, hot, fever-discredited Rome, and this circumstance, together with other practical difficulties in getting settled, helped to make it seem that the unrest around us would not cease and the foreignness lay with the weight of homelessness upon us. Add to this that Rome (if one does not yet know it) has an oppressingly sad effect for the first few days: through the lifeless and doleful museum atmosphere it exhales, through the abundance of its pasts, fetched-forth and laboriously upheld pasts (on which a small present subsists), through the immense overestimation, sustained by savants and philologists and copied by the average traveler in Italy, of all these disfigured and dilapidated things, which at bottom are after all no more than chance remains of another time and of a life that is not and must not be ours. Finally, after weeks of being daily on the defensive, one finds oneself again, if still somewhat confused, and one says to oneself: no, there is not *more* beauty here than elsewhere, and all these objects, continuously admired by generations and patched and mended by workmen's hands, signify nothing, are nothing, and have no heart and no value;—but there

is much beauty here, because there is much beauty everywhere. Waters unendingly full of life move along the old aqueducts into the great city and dance in the many squares over white stone basins and spread out in wide spacious pools and murmur by day and lift up their murmuring to the night that is large and starry here and soft with winds. And gardens are here, unforgettable avenues and flights of stairs, stairs devised by Michelangelo, stairs that are built after the pattern of downward-gliding waters—broadly bringing forth step out of step in their descent like wave out of wave. Through such impressions one collects oneself, wins oneself back again out of the pretentious multiplicity that talks and chatters there (and how talkative it is!), and one learns slowly to recognize the very few things in which the eternal endures that one can love and something solitary in which one can quietly take part.[1]

Among the ruins and the tired objects of an ancient city, there is a beauty that resonates in the soul because it speaks of how the "eternal endures" rarely in our world, but that love finds such things and sits before them, quietly and alone, in glowing adoration.

I come to this city again and again precisely to locate such moments of quiet and adoration. I seek to find the fullness of my own being within them, to become lost in the act of rejoicing that such eternal moments produce within me as well.

Every true voyage has the possibility to turn into a pilgrimage, because every voyage starts with the restless longing to connect with something out of the ordinary—even if I do not know at times why I am restless, why I desire to leave my home for parts and experiences unknown. There is only a decisive expectation that arrives to me from out of nowhere, whose origin I cannot locate or explain, that propels me forward and pushes me to confront that which I have never confronted before.

It is a compelling moment of personal growth each time that seems to originate from beyond me, one in which all of my infinite brokenness, shattered dreams, and those fevered delusions and breathless desires that comprise who I am, become a shadow that enters behind me as I cross the desolate thresholds of a thousand sacred spaces.

---

1. Rilke, *Letters to a Young Poet*, 41–43.

Sacred Pilgrim, Secular Pilgrim

By the time the Grand Tours started in earnest around the middle of the seventeenth century, allowing educated young men from England to obtain a liberal education gathered from the travels and items collected throughout their European adventures, the transformation of the pilgrim into the tourist, or the "student of history," as it was understood by many at the time, had begun. Culture and art soon supplanted religion as the foremost interests of those seeking for more than what they could hold before their eyes, for a road map to the interior journeys of humankind.[2]

Even devout pilgrims departing centuries before such tours took on a certain popularity, those with organized guides from the ports of Venice, received enough direction from their chaperones—including paperwork guaranteeing safe passage that would foreshadow the modern-day passport—to begin a blurring of identities.

When pilgrims began returning from selected routes to Jerusalem and Rome with various artifacts and souvenirs that held a certain appeal of their own, the passion for collecting sacred relics slowly began to replicate itself in new domains.

Within such historical developments, the migration from pilgrim to tourist, and from holy relic to personally meaningful souvenir, became part of those larger processes of secularization that characterized many such trends: the sacred aura of religious figures, such as the pope, gave way to the modern cult of celebrity; religious sites morphed into museums, leaving little that was previously deemed holy unscathed in this complete revaluation of values.

※

Accompanying all of these changes was the sense that meaning itself had somehow suffered at the hands of an unyielding and often invisible desecration. The sacred was no longer sacrosanct. Something had been irredeemably lost and it was not clear that anything had come to take its place.

Despite the fervent discipleship of many in the nineteenth century, for example, poetry and art had not entirely replaced religious commitment. Perhaps there was a certain part of one's humanity that felt touched by the aesthetic nature of existence, but poetry and art were not the whole-scale replacement many had thought they might become.

2. Taylor, Rinne, and Kostof, *Rome*, 303–12.

Yet, if one realizes how the main problem was not simply a one-to-one substitution of art replacing religion, but rather the shattering of a oneness, or a sense of unity itself that left humanity scrambling to locate myriads of alternatives to a variety of religious practices, then perhaps the arts could be seen to replace at least some of what religion had once offered. But not everything, for no one thing could any longer make the claims that religion had once made upon so much of humanity.

༄

Pilgrims from the north entered the eternal city through an ancient Roman gate, the Porta Flaminia, opening onto what is now the Piazza del Popolo. They were first welcomed there by a sumptuous park, an Egyptian obelisk, and a host of churches.

Pilgrims from the south arrived on the Via Appia and entered through an imposing gate, the Porta Appia, now known as the Porta San Sebastiano. Having made such long journeys to Rome, it must have come as quite some relief for pilgrims to be within the city's walls, symbolically, at least, within its protection.

༄

I found myself today stepping in the opposite direction, departing from the city, exiting through its southern gate and making the long trek to the catacombs that lie along the Via Appia Antica as it snakes out far beyond the city. I was putting myself at a remove from the familiar patterns and routines that the visitor to a new city soon falls into, and opening myself to a bit of what lies beyond the city's walls.

The catacombs of S. Callisto and S. Sebastiano—my destinations for the morning—are an immersion into the longing of the early Christian world, to be near one's loved ones, especially after their death. By partaking with them *in* their death, in fact, one could reflect on the saint's journey toward their beloved Christ.

Beyond the rough-hewn tombs cut from the volcanic tufa rock, there are altars placed within certain chambers that indicate just how devoted the faithful were to celebrating their savior alongside their closest family members, past and present. To celebrate life and death as they came together at such points in time and space was one of the highlights of an early Christian's life in Rome, a reality reflected in the fact that the Catholic Church still grants an indulgence to pilgrims who travel to Rome just to visit, and perhaps celebrate mass within, the catacombs.

☙

The catacombs, as I walk underground through them, become a reminder of my own mortality and the choices I have made to live my life as I have lived it. They are, for this reason, not always a welcomed experience.

It is in such places that my disillusionments with life and the disappointments I harbor become that much larger than I generally observe. At the same time as they call me to take note of my impending death, they also prod me to live a life more worthy—to harness my potential and to achieve that which I desire.

There is of course no way to fully reconcile myself to all the choices I have made throughout my life, many of which I inevitably regret. Given another chance, I would not make some of the same decisions again.

Finding peace within the complexity of who I am, however, and so honoring my life in its entirety, means learning to accept my life as I now find it. To do so is to accept my destiny, as it were, the narrative that comprises my biography and to live from such a viewpoint as if without any regrets at all. There is a peace that follows from such an acceptance, though I wonder most days if I will ever really know it in its purest form.

☙

Present-day pilgrims and tourists alike arrive at the catacombs by the busload in order to be returned to this former age and its burial practices. I am often curious about how much a person can be emotionally moved by the experience of being in the catacombs while being led on a tour with at least a dozen other tourists and pilgrims, but the possibility for such an experience still permeates each visit I make.

There is something profoundly foundational to one's faith in walking through these underground cemeteries, and I continue to unpack whatever that lingering sensibility is, as it might apply to my own life.

To be surrounded by the Christian faithful in their eternal rest was, and still is, the basis for the bodies of saints, or at least their relics, being placed under altars in a church. For centuries, to be a church in the official sense meant that the body of a saint, or some part of them, was interred under an altar, bringing their holy presence somehow to life in the center of a religious community's gathering.

The catacombs, in a more original way, reflect the intentions of this practice, allowing one to see just how meaningful it is to be grounded in faith by those faithful who have gone before them.

I have lived for some years now feeling relatively disconnected from my own memories, as if they were someone else's memories and not my own. Experiencing trauma or some major dislocation from a former life, from the familiar patterns and ways that had characterized one's sense of self in the past, erects an opaque sheet of glass between the present and the past.

I had been dislocated from the life I had wanted to live and was left to wander through an unorganized, and seemingly endless, series of disconnected images, stories, and memories that haunted my present, but which could not be used as a foundation for my present self.

Without this foundational sense of my own memory, it has often been difficult to build up a strong sense of self, to lay claim to my stories, to own the words I write or to find purpose and meaning the way it had once seemed to come to easily to me.

Living in this state while undertaking a pilgrimage at times heightens the feelings of alienation, as if I am drifting toward nothing in particular and as if I will continue to drift like this without end.

But I am also aware that, should I refuse to quit the journey and if I learn to surrender to the ambiguity and confusion of the pilgrimage I am making, I can encounter brilliant moments of insight, joy, even rapture, should I let them all in. I walk on in a state of hope that is certainly ephemeral, even though it is also the basis of how I am learning to construct myself anew through the journey I am undertaking.

For years I wanted my faith life to be a expedition that had a definitive ending. I wanted to fall in love with God and live "happily ever after." This child's embrace of a storybook ending was, I later discovered, not actually how faith—or romance—worked. There are depths and detours to such treks, so many that it becomes impossible to say when a trip like this will end. There is only an openness to ambiguity and obscurity that I continuously have to learn to embrace.

Accepting this reality likewise means embracing an inner landscape where I will never embody a state entirely at peace with my faith or my lack of it, even as I sit in moments of solitude and silence and find other experiences of peace than I had ever imagined were possible.

I find tranquility in such moments by letting go of the quest for certainty and solidity in my faith in what I do not comprehend, what will always exceed the boundaries of my understanding. There is a great sublime beauty in recognizing my own failure to express anything of substance when I face this abyss of the impossible within me.

Along an Ancient Road

He wanders along the Via Appia—He reflects on how life and death intersect and overlap—He reflects on the contrast between papal processions and the path of the pilgrim—He feels the loss of the original intent of pilgrimage

THE MOMENT I STEP onto the path running from S. Callisto to S. Sebastiano, it hits me: my heart is elevated more than in any space outside the city walls because it is here that I see both nature and history unfolding before my eyes more fully. The sumptuous greens of the trees lining the road, the golden fields swaying in the breeze to my right, the hedges of light and shadow playing in a subtle rhythm all their own and the occasional burst of color from a budding flower—these give the impression of being miraculous in the most ordinary of ways.

I suspect this is just nature's way of indicating to me that it is implicated in how I comport myself in this world, here as anywhere.

I try as often as possible to visit the mountains of Colorado, to fish in local rivers south of Chicago, where I currently live, to hike nature trails in Wisconsin, and to go as often as possible to see the cornfields of my home state of Illinois move like a green wave across the prairie.

These places are sacred sites to me, without need of an explanation or justification of any sort. No indulgences are granted me for these visits, except the ones that seem to be given to me the moment I arrive. It is odd and yet wholly natural that humanity creates so many sites that it then designates as sacred. These natural ones predate us, will most likely outlast us, and they carry a power that we will never fully comprehend.[1]

---

1. On the paths of nature as potential sites of pilgrimage, see, among others, Macfarlane, *Old Ways*.

It is more than possible, indeed it is very likely, that my quest to understand the intentions of the true pilgrim is really a journey of returning to a respect for the oldest sacred sites of them all: the natural beauty and wonder of the landscapes that surround us.

It strikes me like an epiphany, this understanding that all I have been seeking to cultivate as a secular pilgrim is a respect for the tensions and silences that abound everywhere around me and within me—a willingness to enter and sit beside the mysteries I will never understand, a desire to maintain the beauty, complexity, and even poverty of life that teems all around me.

All of these moments point toward a willingness to sit in the various ecospheres I live within and to recognize the transcendent power of whatever lives, breathes, and moves in them. I will never fully grasp what makes the smallest organism tick or how it interacts with the large-scale life-forms around it, but I do not need to know. I need only to recognize that I am a pilgrim in this world, needing to listen better, walk more gently throughout each space, and be much more attentive to the rhythms and differences that permeate our shared existence.

✧

This ancient path of the pilgrim along the Via Appia goes right by the catacombs and is further lined with tombs and funerary monuments, strange but familiar ways to be reminded of how life and death intersect and overlap in the midst of the busiest routes we take on this planet.

Life and death are locked in an inescapable tension that nature presents us with, and accepting this reality means also accepting what is most fundamental about our existence.

There is no path for the pilgrim that is pure or free of distractions and the temptation to abandon the pilgrimage altogether. The temptation to end the wandering is always there, just as death haunts our every living moment. But this inescapable tension is also the source of our humanity, just as it constantly shapes our thoughts and insights about how we live our lives.

There is no purity in the pilgrimage, just as there is also no true corruption of it. Faith, like love, works much the same way.

We humans leave nature in order to form our own artificial worlds, what we call society or civilization. And religion has always been essential to the glue that holds us together. We create sacred spaces within our communities to remind us of what we left behind and so too of the awareness and reverence for life that we seek to maintain but which eludes us most days.

The sacred calls us back to such an attentiveness of these presences that actually are around us all of the time. So many spiritual masters, like the poet Mary Oliver, for example, often feel a tension between finding God in a religious and socially recognized context and finding the divine in nature. If sacred spaces exist to remind us of our nature, however, then there really is no division here: both point toward our affinity with nature because we are part of nature, always called to reconnect to our humanity, which is really another form of our being an animal.

I feel the grasses along the Via Appia with my hands and scenes from my childhood flash through my mind. They carry me to a place of security and wonder, places I am searching for still and that call to me through my memories. I am grateful to be greeted by them again, if only for a passing moment.

There is at the heart of Christianity an experience of atheism that I embrace and lift up as my own personal testament. At the end of each Gospel, God dies, and, in two of those Gospels at least, he cries out about the lack of divine presence that he feels.

It would be a blatant misreading of the Gospel message to deny the loss of faith in one's image of God, that which so boldly accompanies the death of Christ on the cross. Why the Christian should balk at the label of atheist, as one who feels the absence of God acutely, baffles me still and confounds the wisdom of the "crucified God" that Christianity professes to follow.

As I look at the many crucifixes that adorn the walls behind the many altars of Rome, I often wonder if the truest experience of faith in Jesus' divinity is to renounce my own faith in God altogether. There is no pride in such gestures, only the recognition that our greatest strength sometimes shines through in our greatest weaknesses.

I believe that Jesus taught humanity this lesson quite well.

I have no desire to be heretical in saying this, no urge to rebel against the beauty and passion that religious devotion can inspire, no ill will toward those who are devoutly religious, and no desire to deviate from the mystical heart of understanding how little we truly understand of both ourselves and anything that could truly be called sacred.

※

While praying in the catacombs under San Sebastiano sometime in the sixteenth century, St. Philip Neri felt his heart expand to twice its normal size, a fact seemingly confirmed by an autopsy after his death. His being so moved by the love of God, it is easy to imagine why this church in particular held a special place for him among the pilgrim churches of Rome, a list he himself defined.

Located along the scenic entryway to the city, the Via Appia, the church and catacombs of San Sebastiano were once the resting place for the remains, or relics, of both saints Peter and Paul. Though their relics were later moved to the individual basilicas in Rome bearing their names, this church especially held a unique appeal for pilgrims because of its historical and global prominence.

Neri himself eventually added this church to his small list of the seven pilgrim churches in Rome, or just outside of its walls—each a reminder to the pilgrim of a station along the route of Jesus' passion.

Neri and the other devout worshippers he organized into a group would walk to each of the seven churches within the span of a single day, performing a tiny pilgrimage within the city that still helped the faithful to experience the fruits of pilgrimage for themselves. Forming something of an informal pilgrimage route, this path has been emulated many times over throughout the years, and it is one I often take when in town.[2]

---

2. Neri's original list of the seven pilgrim churches includes S. Giovanni in Laterano (St. John Lateran), S. Pietro (St. Peter's), S. Paolo fuori le mura (St. Paul Outside the Walls), S. Maria Maggiore (St. Mary Major), S. Lorenzo fuori le mura (St. Lawrence Outside the Walls), Santa Croce in Gerusalemme (Holy Cross in Jerusalem), and S. Sebastiano fuori le mura (St. Sebastian Outside the Walls), which was subsequently replaced in 1999 by Our Lady of Divine Love shrine by Pope John Paul II.

The original basilica of San Sebastiano was built around 340, and a newer, smaller basilica was built in the seventeenth century over the catacombs, where in fact St. Sebastian himself had been buried. Early in the church's history, additional relics from the Christian community in Rome may also have been brought here for safekeeping, making this site a frequent one for pilgrims, especially in the medieval period. Larger basilicas were built over time above these relics to accommodate the increasing number of pilgrims who would visit, eventually resulting in the church of San Sebastiano as it is known today.

The presence of such relics, along with those of Peter and Paul, elevated San Sebastiano to one of the original seven pilgrim churches, though it is less visited today and not kept up as well as the others (and was even replaced by John Paul II as a pilgrim church in favor of a modern, popularized Marian shrine).

☙

Saint Sebastian himself was an early martyr (d. 288) who was tied to a tree and shot with arrows, though miraculously he survived and was nursed back to health by Saint Irene of Rome. His attempts to convince the Roman Emperor Diocletian to stop persecuting Christians did not go well, however, and he was subsequently clubbed to death.

The church contains the remains of St. Sebastian as well as the "Quo vadis" slab, which bears essentially the alleged imprints of Jesus' feet when he miraculously appeared to Peter on the Via Appia, asking Peter "where are you going?" as the latter fled the city and those seeking to arrest him.

This story may have been part of the Roman Church's efforts to demonstrate the centrality of the bishop, and Church, of Rome to the rest of Christendom at a later date—a point that was emphasized through the Roman Church's increasing ecclesial rank, suggesting that it was the authority in all matters Christian throughout the world.

☙

A general Christian belief in the resurrection of the dead led to a prohibition on cremation in the Church and so too arose the necessity of preserving the bodies of the deceased. Feast days of the martyrs were celebrated near their tombs in the catacombs and the persecution of Christians in the third century created many martyrs in Rome who were then celebrated at their final resting place in the catacombs.

Pope Damasus (d. 384) was the one who really built up and preserved the catacombs. He was also the pope who established the papal archives to provide another foundational point for the early church's sense of itself. The catacombs of S. Callisto nearby contain a room of the earliest popes' tombs, starting in 250, which is when papal succession really begins.

The room was a place for celebrating liturgies and is even where some popes were arrested for being Christian and executed on the spot. Pope Callixtus I was the one who started the catacombs here, but he himself was not buried on site. He was killed by a popular uprising in the Trastevere region of Rome in 222, perhaps due to Christians encroaching upon territory in an otherwise overcrowded area.[3] S. Maria in Trastevere was his main church and it is one that I will have reason to speak of later.

Studying the figures of the two pilgrims ensconced in near darkness in Caravaggio's painting "Madonna of the Pilgrims" located in Sant'Agostino near the Piazza Navona, one gains a vision of humility and poverty in human form, as if one were capable of presenting more than their exterior selves to the Queen of Heaven before whom these pilgrims kneel.

The image is particularly striking in the contrast it maintains between the inner and outer poverty of the true pilgrim and the tourist spectacles that often characterize those making the journey to Rome.

Neri's simple route to each of the seven churches in Rome, contrasted with the many regal, papal processions throughout the city over the centuries, which conveyed an imperial might that the pilgrim would violently shun, mirror the former tension. Boulevards had been widened and buildings knocked down in order to make way for traditional papal processions as they wound their way throughout the city, though such grandiose gestures leave one to wonder whether the original intent of pilgrimage had been somewhat lost in such displays.

The importance of the routes and the processions that took place along them—such as the Via Papalis connecting the Vatican to the Lateran—were

---

3. Duffy, *Saints and Sinners*, 19.

that they displaced and absorbed the Roman triumphal processions, moments in history when Roman emperors would parade their conquered enemies in a show of military and political strength.[4]

The papal procession eventually became on its own a display of sovereign power, with all the pageantry one could imagine.[5] With Christianity's ascension to power in Rome came the desire to conquer the conquerors themselves, to outdo the dominance of the Roman empire through a display of Christ's kingship over the entire world, something that the *globus cruciger*, or orb with a cross on top of it often placed atop the basilicas of Rome and others throughout the world, would attempt to proclaim to the rest of humanity.

ஐ

I am struck by how much the tensions and influences of the world threaten to undermine the pilgrim's interior journey, though I am never shocked. Such tensions will not go away and will always be there to remind us of what else in this world lays claim upon us.

Finding a way to navigate through such circumstances and still maintain one's orientation toward the deepest parts of themselves becomes a significant part of the pilgrim's task as well.

ஐ

The Domine Quo Vadis ("Lord, Where Are You Going?") Church on the Via Appia pays homage to the legendary story of Peter's conversation with a post-resurrection Jesus who appeared to be headed back to Rome to be crucified a second time while Peter was fleeing the city to avoid his own arrest and potential martyrdom. Peter, upon seeing a vision of Christ, got the message and turned around to face his destiny within the city he was trying to escape.

Jesus' sudden and miraculous disappearance apparently left an impression on Peter, but also on the stone under his feet, for Jesus was said to have left his footprints behind according to legend. Though the original stone impressions are retained on display at S. Sebastiano, this church

4. Taylor, Rinne, and Kostof, *Rome*, 156.
5. Taylor, Rinne, and Kostof, *Rome*, 272.

marks the purported site where the exchange was said to have taken place and a replica of his footprints resides here as well.

❧

The images of fleeing one's destiny, fleeing a will imposed upon one's life, is a difficult one to absorb. Though I do not wish to see the will of God as an imposition, there are many who have fashioned their theology toward a sovereign sense of predestination that appears to dictate the coordinates and conditions of one's entire life. Though I find such ideas repellent, I am also well aware of the feeling that my life has been "fated" to head in a certain direction at certain points, wholly beyond my control.

I wonder at times if pilgrimage is an escape from one's circumscribed life and so if it is a carnivalesque suspension of the daily routine so that one can simply return to it at a later date. But I am also aware enough of the fact that there are times when we are confronted by realities beyond our comprehension that do more than just suspend our normal existence.

There *are* profound moments of epiphany that we experience, like Peter's vision of Christ, that alter the conditions of material reality itself.

I would be lying if I said that I wasn't at times desperate for such transformations to take place, what the biblical account refers to as transfigurations of one's being. We all need such out-of-the-ordinary moments to awaken us and to grant to us a sense that life could be otherwise than how we live it, could be better, fuller, and so much richer than we could've ever imagined it to be.

❧

I return to Rome often to declare my lack of belief in God to God, to have God bear witness to my atheism, to reconceive of the Catholicism I once adopted in my twenties by inverting its image to myself so that I might see more depth in myself and others than I had ever seen before.

I return to Rome to protest this loss of faith and to ignore it, ultimately to become indifferent to it.

I return to Rome to stand immersed in something much larger than myself, the tradition, buildings, and rituals of Roman Catholicism, to rediscover, to struggle and to relent in the face of the myriad tensions that crisscross the streets and bodies I come across each hour, as they reflect back to me the complexity of the mystery that I remain to myself.

My inability at times to tell the difference between myself and the other before me becomes the only goal, until I dissolve into the holiness of such moments.

The Material Nature of Faith

He finds tension between a loss of meaning and new experiences of modern art—He recognizes connections between art and spiritual insight—The tourist and the pilgrim as the same person—He feels the pilgrim's unwillingness to embrace poverty—He affirms that to know God is to know that one does not know much about God

QUITE A NUMBER OF Roman churches have found ways to commemorate material moments of faith, such as the miracle of the lost keys to the cathedral of Meissen, Germany being returned by a fisherman who found them inside a fish he had caught, a story which is prominently displayed in a side chapel painting at S. Maria dell'Anima just off the Piazza Navona in Rome.

Even the disembodied, fragmented forms of modern art and poetry overlap with this fetishistic side of religious materiality.

Art, for its part, should never try to remove itself from this truth. When art, for example, exhibits itself as if removed from the religious symbolic networks of meaning that had dominated our understanding of art for centuries in the West, it still isolates a particular point of view or experience, and uplifts this isolated element as a value (fetish) in and of itself.

This reality of course explains why pop art, with its links to the commodity fetish, as Marx had termed it, can be commercialized so easily. Detached from any larger network of meaning—as modern art and atheism are both characterized—it is easy to focus on form and shape only, devoid of any placement in a larger narrative, as abstract art revels in promoting. Abstract art, in this sense, is made possible by the decline in religious narratives and traditions.

The popularity of being spiritual but not religious today stems from this same abstraction and devotion to the shape of religion without religion actually being there. To look at a piece of modern art and wonder what exactly it is or what it should even mean is by definition the point of its existence.

So much modern art plays with the destruction of those larger symbolic networks of meaning and the ruins or fragments that we are left with as a result. Cultural and personal memories are distorted or played with as we witness the disintegration of those traditions that humanity has held dear for so long.

For the traditionally religious individual or community, this stripping of tradition to only its shape and form can be a disastrous loss of meaning and value. But for the more modern sensibility, it is a chance to locate something new about ourselves beyond what we have recognized and known thus far. This tension will not be easily resolved and it haunts us at the moment still quite profoundly.

ೃ

I too have had the experience of viewing some modern, abstract art and wondering what it was about, if too much hadn't been lost in the rush to deconstruct every existing tradition, authority, institution, or narrative. But I've also experienced the epiphany of seeing the abstractions of form point back toward reality, depicting the world before me in new ways that did nothing short of expand my mind well beyond what I could've ever imagined.

One time at a Cy Twombly retrospective at the Pompidou Center in Paris, I finally "got" his art when I saw so many of his canvases together in one place. The scribbles and geometric shapes that so many dismiss as childlike scratches on a canvas seemed to craft an entire landscape or horizon of meaning that functioned like an x-ray of the reality before me.

My own dismissive reaction to his art completely melted away and I was overcome with a profound moment of intuitive connection to what I saw. Seeing his art became a religious experience, one that I take with me wherever I go. For that moment, the fragmentation so often, and rightly, ascribed to contemporary art was reversed and reality shone clear, bathing life all around me in bright, white light.

The journey I took that day, from fragmentation to a vision of the whole of reality is precisely what religious mystics have sought and spoken about for centuries, albeit in a different vocabulary and context. It is a shame that religious institutions often miss the similarities and parallels between modern art and spiritual insight when they condemn modern trends in general. A powerful connection is lost in such dismissive attitudes and judgments, no less among the secular despisers of religion as among the religious critics of modern art.

I rest confident that some within the Church *do* recognize such connections, especially perhaps those at Santa Maria in Vallicella in Rome, or the Chiesa Nuova as it's mainly called, where a plaque commemorating Twombly is to be found. Twombly had lived in Rome, died there, and found himself improbably immortalized alongside the bodies and relics of many other saints throughout the city.

I felt more than a tinge of synchronicity in my journey when I discovered his memorial accidently while walking through the Chiesa Nuova one sunny afternoon.

෴

There was no mistaking the uncanny feeling of hollowness, however, when I stepped through the single entranceway just inside the steel grillwork of a portico, and slightly disappointing atmosphere, of San Pietro in Vincoli, or Saint Peter in Chains. Though it is a Roman church dating back to the fifth century, it is now in need of some amount of restoration and it seems to desperately search for a sense of itself, caught as it is between trying to meet the needs of both pilgrim and tourist at the same time.

A painting on the ceiling of the church tells of the miracle that supposedly took place when the two chains said to have held Saint Peter in prison, and so also the two legends they carried with them, were brought together and miraculously joined into a single chain. It seems more wishful thinking than reality, but this miracle, regarded to have taken place around the mid-fifth century, was meant to dispel all doubts as to the relic's authenticity.

So that there might be no uncertainty about the miracle's genuineness, the painting also shows how the pope healed a goiter on the neck of an afflicted woman by touching her with these holy chains.

The Material Nature of Faith

The credulity-straining history of the chains is overburdened by the presence of what were said to be the remains of the seven Maccabean brothers and subsequent martyrs which were placed under the main altar in the sixth century. In the 1930s, it was revealed that what lay within the box were actually dog bones and so ultimately a hoax perpetrated upon unsuspecting Christians, but what baffles the mind further is how these remains have not been removed, with a discreet label still indicating that the brothers' remains are indeed located there.

The crypt, however, is now kept locked and not much notice is paid to it by those casually perusing the area just under the main altar.

Though the relics in the *confessio* are what the religious pilgrim searches for, most of the small crowd who enter the church actually come to see Pope Julius II's failed tomb project for St. Peter's, which in 1545 had grown so out of proportion for that particular site that its façade was relocated here. More specifically, it is not Pope Julius II that people come to pay their respects to, especially considering how Julius was one of the more scandalous Renaissance popes as he lived an extremely worldly life. (He had three daughters illegitimately and was often seen wearing silver armor into battle against his enemies, though he was also patron to the artists Raphael, Bramante, and Michelangelo. Julius was moreover the pope who laid the foundation stone for the modern St. Peter's Basilica, under the architectural guidance of Bramante.)

What people come to see on the forefront of his tomb is Michelangelo's resplendent sculpture of Moses.

The sculpture has become somewhat famous since the "horns" on his head are based on a mistranslation of the Hebrew phrase "rays of light," which was rendered as "horns" in the Latin Vulgate. This is a mistranslation parallel, some might say, to the mistranslation of a "young woman" said to give birth to a son in the prophet Isaiah's Scripture, to the translation of "young woman" becoming "virgin" in the Greek—a point the authors of the Christian Gospels were quick to demonstrate was fulfilled in Jesus' miraculous birth. (For many today who hear this story for the first time, the mistranslation seems to share the same fate as the dog bones under the main altar in this church. Jesus' virgin birth seems to have been revealed as a fabrication, but there the story sits nonetheless.)

❧

The presence of Michelangelo's Moses is the most significant draw for visitors to San Pietro in Vincoli today, though its presence begs a number of questions concerning the relationship between church and museum, as most visitors here are clearly tourists and not pilgrims. For a church that had once been considered a possible eighth pilgrimage church in Rome—among the seven that were officially labeled as such—this is an interesting, and perhaps problematic, juxtaposition, especially considering the presence of Peter's chains just a few feet away from the statue.

The pilgrim has been secularized into the tourist, who still potentially displays the same awe and reverence, keeping silence in front of the sacred—except that the sacred space they journey to is the museum and not the church. The papers, guaranteeing safe travel to the pilgrim, and first issued in Venice to those seeking to travel to the Holy Land, become passports; relics become souvenirs; and reliquaries once used to house sacred objects become Wunderkammers or "cabinets of curiosity," before subsequently taking the form of museums.

In these transitions and translations, the supernatural is transformed into the merely "exotic" and "foreign," while the desire to reach out and touch what lies wholly beyond our comprehension remains the same—a longing for what was out of the ordinary, for what could remove one from their ordinary life.

The combination of the material and the spiritual that identifies the relic also identifies the work of art, as both traverse the terrain of the sacrament and the fetish.[1] The value of relics, once the expensive treasures of monarchs, becomes the overinflated artworks of the modern era. To simply be in the presence of a Van Gogh or a Monet painting becomes for some the equivalent of touching the robes of a Saint Francis of Assisi or the bones of saints Peter and Paul.

❧

1. I explore this theme much more in-depth in my book *Fetish of Theology*.

The Material Nature of Faith

Our world in the modern period may seem to be increasingly secular, but our all-too-human impulses remain much the same, taking the tourist on the most remote journeys in order to provide access to what the pilgrim had once also sought: an exceeding of the ordinary as a transcendent experience, a touching of what the everyday cannot provide, and an inner trip to the core of one's own being as a creature meant to find itself only when it is able to go beyond itself.

The tourist and the pilgrim are not just similar, then, they are in fact one and the same person. Understanding this conjunction and transformation might help us to renew the soul of the tourist today, who has become spiritually hollow, devoid of the pilgrim's depth, a shallow manifestation of the pilgrim's inner explorative desire.

All too often these days, the tourist does not understand their own need to travel, just as they do not understand the inner depths they are looking to explore and cultivate. There is only a fleeting encounter with one's depths, hastily brought about by the ease of global travel, the impossibility of comprehending the means by which they arrive at their destination (increasingly through cars and flights) and a luxurious experimental side, with an industry built conveniently around it, that seeks mainly to divert the tourist from encountering any depth whatsoever within themselves.

The focus has been displaced from inner journey of personal and spiritual transformation to a schema of pleasure, relaxation, and distraction.

It is for this reason that so many people take trips around the world while lacking any real insight about what it is that they are doing or what it is that they are even chasing after. They confuse the destination with the goal of the trip, which is inner transformation, and they return from their travels exhausted rather than refreshed. Or they simply add each destination to a weary list of "countries I've visited around the world."

The advent of cameras, social media, and endless distractions in the palm of one's hands have only worsened matters, though each of these things is not inherently bad in and of themselves.

What has been lost sight of is the pilgrim's willingness to renounce, that is, to embrace the poverty that brings about an openness to whatever sacred presence stands before them. Learning to inject travel and tourism today with a renewed capacity for depth will not be brought about by a new marketing campaign. It will only take place through the effort of each individual committed to the pilgrim's methods and means, as meager and intense as they are.

Sacred Pilgrim, Secular Pilgrim

Pilgrimage is not something to be achieved, nor is it something to simply offset our normal goals for success in the world. The temptation to utilize pilgrimage as a vacation or as a means to balance out one's normally hectic-paced life is to miss the point of the potential for transformation that the pilgrim undergoes.

To be a pilgrim is to allow oneself to be altered, transformed completely, taken from one way of life to another, not simply to refresh us so that we might return to the drudgery of our normal routines.

※

Among the pilgrims and the relics—those real, fake, and unsubstantiated—and the tourists crossing the marble floors of San Pietro in Vincoli, the hollow feeling continues to overcome me, and my desire to face it grows with equal intensity.

No matter how one tries to defend Christianity and its doctrinal claims, a more and more secular world devoid of religious sentiment is advancing upon the West, and its narrative is overtaking those apologists who desperately plead for the relevance of the religious. Christianity, and religion generally, has much to offer to humanity in terms of the insights and wisdom that it has accrued over the millennia, but it is also suspended in what appears to be a dying state as a new secular space free from dogmatic belief allows multiple narratives to coexist simultaneously without the express need to have any one, singular narrative dominate over any other. There is no essence to humanity, no end goal to which we are oriented and, despite the fears that many express over this state of things, this contingency actually allows for more creative expressions and for new freedoms that many have never known before.

There is also a responsibility that we bear in this freedom and that we have to discover along the many paths we walk along.

※

What, in the meantime, will it mean for religion to embrace its own poverty? What will become of these sacred spaces turned into museums and art repositories? Will we still be able to experience an epiphany in them?

The Material Nature of Faith

Will we try to turn our epiphany into a new religion or find another way to cultivate the truths that are being spoken to us?

It should be religious persons who are the most comfortable with the ambiguity in which we now sit, since one's proximity to any alleged divinity would have to provoke not only a sense of utter humility about one's knowledge and one's limitations, but would necessarily entail as well a certain comfortability with residing next to, even at the heart of, a mystery that engulfs us all.

The divine, it has been presumed by most religions, is ultimately unknowable and certainly far beyond the reach of the human mind. To know God, it might be said, is to know mainly that one does not know much about God at all. This is the summit of insight for a religious knowledge that is generally considered to be a negative form of knowing—historically the domain of mystical speech known as negative theology. It is the route most mystics walk down because their desire to stand so close to the divine presence means that they are somewhat blinded, perhaps even blinded completely, by the supposed immensity of God's majesty.

There is a state of unknowing that the devout enter when they stand exposed to the divine presence, though it is a state of humility often not shared by those religious persons or groups who seek not to remain in the ambiguous presence of mystery (also referred to as a *sacrament* in Greek), but seek rather to mobilize believers as a political collective in order to make gains for themselves in this world.

It seems as if most of us would rather enter new levels of distraction and material possession than to face the uncertainty that resides permanently embedded within our very existence.

Ongoing Distractions

He enters S. Maria in Arcaelae and S. Lorenzo in Lucina—He witnesses the storm of modern consumerism among the tourists—He hopes the immeasurable value of silence in the midst of it all can be preserved—Keeping focus, resolve, and seriousness about the journey being made

CAPITALIST CONSUMERISM IS THE real religion worshipped these days in Rome, or at least it is the one with the greatest claim made upon most of the city's visitors. To craft one's social media image while dining on a resplendent piazza after hours of shopping and sightseeing is its own form of worship. To simply "have gone" to Rome and to partake in its global brand is to satisfy some vague longing to have acquired or possessed the experience of Rome, all without actually experiencing much substance.

In truth, the city is filled with insoluble tensions between global consumerism, Catholic traditions, ancient Roman history, Italian nationalist memories and monuments, and the city's darker undercurrent of immigrants and poverty, which remain the inseparable reverse side of its current global, capitalist phase. The beauty of the city is often at odds with the graffiti and general unkemptness of the streets, a reality reflected by the abundant dirtiness and trash palpable almost everywhere.

And yet, as I reflected while descending from the Villa Borghese to the heart of the city, seeing the rooftops and church steeples from above, these things are also a reminder of how much there is to love about the complexity and depth of Rome. To steal an intimate moment like this amidst all the tourists and noise can be a treasure to receive in the midst of any circumstance.

Ongoing Distractions

It is abundantly clear after less than an hour of walking through Rome that the churches are mainly utilized as tourist attractions for visitors to the city. The buildings are treated like museums and the scores of photographers snapping pictoral souvenirs seem so opposed to the spiritual efforts of the pilgrim.

It could of course be argued that the photograph becomes a relic in its own right to many, a reminder of the journey itself that transports one backwards in time and allows for another experience of pilgrimage to emanate from the twin distances of time and place.

There will always be a tension between the willingness to let oneself become fully immersed in a moment and the photographic desire to establish a semipermanent distance from the immediacy of the moment. We rest in the sights and symbols that we are immersed in and that carry us with them as much as we carry them with us.

༄

The average museumgoer is probably as little aware of the rich symbolic nature of the art they see as the visitor to a church is aware of the complex religious imagery there on display. Most venture to such places in some sort of fervor looking for a brief glimpse of beauty, and a fleeting communion with something larger than themselves. Few will have an inspiring encounter, to be sure, but the desire for one lies underneath it all.

I am all too aware of the historical fact that Christians once profaned the sacred temples of Roman religion, destroying the altars therein while also consciously transforming these holy sites into city museums.[1] The irony of such a thing happening to Christian churches today is therefore not lost on me.

I recall the Italian philosopher Giorgio Agamben's judgment that the sacred and the secular are often but two sides to the same coin. What we once took in the premodern world to be the vast dominance of the sacred has given way to the secular, which functions much like the sacred once did—what Agamben calls the current experience of an increasing "museification" of our world.[2]

---

1. Taylor, Rinne, and Kostof, *Rome*, 162.
2. Agamben, *Profanations*.

Certain things are set apart, as the sacred once was, though as if now in a museum, untouchable and removed from our immediate experience. They convey a sacred aura in their removal from everyday usage, even if the objects are mundane.

I wonder about this fact when I witness busloads of tourists being shepherded from one holy site to another, unable to break free and roam about, to be lost on purpose and thereby have a more genuine experience of their own. The crowds seem to follow the tour guides and absorb what they are meant to absorb. Their freedom is willingly handed over and one's ability to encounter reality directly dialed back another notch.

How do we acknowledge the desire for something greater than ourselves without settling for the false substitutes that others frequently try to impose on us, both "sacred" and "secular"? How do we learn to stand still before a mysterious presence, external or internal, until we are met by the sublimity we are after?

༄

Perhaps it is due to the daunting climb up so many steps that keeps the crowd reduced in size at S. Maria in Arcaelae, which borders an always crowded central artery for tourists in the city. There are more chandeliers in this church than side chapels, and certainly more than the number of persons here today. An ornate ceiling and sumptuous marble characterize the nave, as do the extremely worn figures on the tombs underfoot.

Quiet descends immediately as a result of being in such a large, empty space, buffered on all sides as if by solitude itself. The church is a refuge at the heart of so much busy activity, laying as it does near the heart of the Forum, the Capitoline museums, and the Altar of the Fatherland.

I treasure experiences like these when I find a space for seclusion along an otherwise busy journey, where few people venture and where space has been made available to me to look inward at my own experiences—experiences of the place I am in and of my inner world at the same time.

Encountering a presence, no matter whether sublime, majestic, or ordinary yet intimate, depends upon my taking the time and finding the patience to first be present to myself and to the environment around me. These spaces of prayer and of hope, whether we recall this fact or treat them as such, were made for such moments within a person's life, when the frenetic activity of the day is suspended by an inner desire for something more—something beyond.

⁂

Later that same day, I sat completely alone in S. Lorenzo in Lucina during what was one of the oddest clashes I have yet experienced inside a Roman church. In the midst of a high shopping street, someone at the church had propped open its main doors so that the music, the passersby, the dining populace on the sidewalks, and the children running in the street outside could all be heard clearly from inside the sanctuary. The nonstop carnival of modern capitalist consumerism threatened to claim victory over whatever meditative forces might still have a place, but the space remained cordoned off as a testament to the value of silence in the midst of it all. This value is immeasurable and a lesson much needed today.

As if on cue, in fact within minutes of my arrival, a woman with three small children entered the church and proceeded to quietly—as quietly as could be imagined with inevitably boisterous small ones—observe some of the artwork and history of the sanctuary. As the woman reminded the children on occasion to be quiet, I felt hope that something of the value of such spaces and the silence they offer amid a busy world might be preserved.

⁂

I cannot deny the frustrations and inconveniences of the touristic hordes occupying the streets of the city; the churches inconveniently under renovation during my stay; the many odd hours of operation that cause me to miss an opportunity at seeing a beautiful interior; being shooed away while in the midst of my reflections because a rosary is starting; having to pay a couple euros to activate the interior lighting in order to see an artistic masterpiece; sections of churches being cordoned off for no ostensible reason, and the like. But I also cannot let these things distract me from the purpose of the pilgrim. The pilgrim works to stay focused no matter what obstacle is present, and the way in which the pilgrim handles such obstacles speaks to how the pilgrim understands themselves and the journey they are on.

I ask myself how I am invited into these moments of potential distraction, to embrace another unexpected experience and I learn to cultivate a sensibility that bends and receives rather than imposes and deflects.

Allowing certain obstacles and distractions to override one's journey may indicate a lack of focus, resolve, or seriousness about the journey they are making. Or it may simply reflect how now is not the right time to undertake such things.

To be able to weather any obstacle and yet to stay focused on the reason for the journey—whatever that reason is, no matter how personal or obscure—is done without much thought for the pilgrim, because they move, grow, and discover as if there were no choice in the matter. The will is fixed on each step taken because the journey itself has become essential to who they are. Only when one is willing to risk themselves entirely, to leave what feels safe and comfortable because they have nothing left to lose anymore—the poverty that must be embraced—can the transformative process of pilgrimage begin. And only then can it have any effect upon a person's state of being as well.

🍃

I can't shake the feeling that it might be better for the spirit of the city if Rome's tourist industry were to collapse and the hordes were to disappear. I share somewhat in the sentiment I see in graffiti on the side of a building near the Colosseum: "Tourists go home."

As I feel too about the medieval city of Florence in Tuscany, I can imagine returning to Rome to experience its magnificent structures and history during the winter so as to be able to be more present, with fewer people around, to encounter whatever I find there.

🍃

The solitude I seek is not unwelcomed. It is the cornerstone of the pilgrim's identity.

I need not be told or reminded to feel that it is perfectly fine to be alone, that it is fine to be lost, that it is human to long for something and to desire it even when these desires seem unable to be satisfied. There is only an apparent contradiction between the image of the pilgrim as one who eventually rests eternal in their true "home" (some version of "heaven") and the nonbeliever who remains in near constant uncertainty but endlessly longs to rest in the experience of love. They are, if seen from the right angle, the same thing.

Just as an encounter with death can allow us to see what we most want from our life, so too can the experience of ourselves, *with* ourselves *in* our aloneness, allow us to know what we want in a relationship. Pilgrimage exercises upon us this lesson in authentic recognition of what really matters.

We are thus taught the true value and worth of our own experiences.

Beyond Pilgrimage, Still a Pilgrim

He visits S. Sabina on the Aventine Hill and wanders through the Testaccio area—He feels more at peace and uplifted when he is away from the "holy sites" and among the populace—The insight comes that no single modern phenomenon can replace religion; only a plurality of practices can form the religious dimensions of human existence—He visits the XII Apostles Church—He affirms the necessity for the pilgrim to encounter the twelve apostles—The uniqueness of Christianity not only in its religious, supernatural claims, but in its philosophical ones

By the time I arrive at S. Sabina's in the late afternoon, it is a most welcome relief to be shorn of the crowds. I had decided to walk from S. Pietro in Vincoli to S. Sabina on the Aventine Hill via the Colosseum just to see what kind of a crowd was idling there today. I was not disappointed. People lingered in the usual shady spots, remained in the typical holding patterns of exhausted tourist and rebuffed street vendor in familiar and brusque ways.

S. Sabina's was, in contrast, a refuge and a haven.

I was, once again, the only person inside the church as soon as I entered. It is no wonder to me that, as I mentioned before, the monk and writer Thomas Merton was so spiritually moved here, in the church where Thomas Aquinas himself had resided for a time, where the architecture closely resembled the oldest patterns for churches in Rome and where one could still find a moment to gather oneself more completely than nearly anywhere else down the hill.

༄

I basked in the silence and bathed in an absence of all thought.

I can understand why Moses, Elijah, and Jesus went to the tops of mountains to receive a word "from above." It isn't just some alleged proximity to the divine that calls to a person from such heights. It is how one is removed from the everyday hustle on the streets and in the work place, how one is able to rise above it all for a moment and to gain a new perspective.

If one is transfigured in these spaces, it is no surprise, for the removal to such a distance is necessary for any type of transformation to occur.

ಜ

After some time, I descended the other side of the hill, and began to wander through the Testaccio region of the city, where, after some minutes, I sat down at an empty bench in the piazza. There were ostensibly no tourists here today, and I felt uplifted to be so secluded from it all.

I wondered too what it meant that I felt more connected and reflective when I was away from the "holy sites" and among the general populace of the city. At times when I visit Rome, I have chosen to stay in those regions that are farther outside of the city center so that I might have room to breathe, to think, and to write.

What does it mean, I wondered, that I felt more at peace away from everything and in the present-day, modern Roman neighborhoods where only the locals seemed to dwell? Was this a sign of my Roman pilgrimages slowly coming to an end? Or was my definition of pilgrimage changing so that the ordinary now became extraordinary as the appeal of the sacred, in its exotic foreignness, started to fade for me?

If Rome ceased to be a holy city for me at some point, I don't think I would be disappointed in the least. I think I would rather have gained something of inestimable value, a new sense of what I wanted, something else to seek somewhere else—other sacred experiences calling to me. Such an experience would merely be a part of the larger quest of letting go of what I had once valued in order to discover a greater openness to that which I face in the immediacy of my days.

ಜ

The Testaccio area provides culture and an openness to contemporary arts while also framing Rome's past against a contemporary backdrop. The

Centrale Montemartini museum, for example, places some of the finest and oldest of Rome's mosaics and sculptures in a former mechanical factory, juxtaposing the old and the new in provocative and thoughtful ways.

Much of contemporary Christian theology contemplates just how it should address the increasingly secular culture in which we live. Much of modern art and poetry, as the poet and insurance company executive Wallace Stevens himself wondered aloud, considers whether it can now replace religion.

Centrale Montemartini, by bypassing Christianity altogether and skipping from ancient to modern periods, embodies something of an answer.

I do not think either art or poetry, taken alone, can replace the multifaceted entity that religion has been throughout the years. But these things can replace parts of religious practice, leaving so many other modern phenomena to replace other aspects of what religion once seemed to solely possess. Therapy, exercise routines, healthy diets, tourism, novels, and so much more all work together to make up the modern equivalents of what religion once offered, though in a much less hegemonic or monolithic fashion. There will be no single, secular substitute for religion, only a plurality of practices that form a composite picture of the religious dimensions of human existence.

At the same time, as this reality unfolds before us and religion fades ever further away, it is nonetheless important to note how few of these secular practices have an inherently moral dimension, except to recognize the need for plurality and difference.

It is here that we can recognize too how Christianity contains a deep moral impetus toward preserving those individuals living their lives on the margins of society, of emphasizing weakness and vulnerability over strength and the goodness of sacrifice and selflessness. These are no minor accomplishments, and must be seen as making a unique contribution to Western and global thought on the whole.

※

Perhaps because I was brought up in the Christian tradition, it has taken nearly all of my life thus far to be able to appreciate the greatness and beauty of Roman art forms. Sculpture, mosaics, and frescos all speak to me of a quiet dignity sought in externalized form that had eluded me for most of my life. There is a peacefulness about sculpture in particular that, though clearly idealizing the body and specific historical and mythological heroic deeds, yet offers us a monument to, and meditation upon, our embodied state of existence.

The clash between the ideals of Greek and Roman sculpture with their perfected bodies and the Christian emphasis on the brokenness of bodies, both human and divine, is stark. Yet Christianity also idealizes humans as the Romans once did too—just think of the stress upon saints and virginal, "pure" bodies, a link so strong that a temple to the Roman Vestal Virgins was later associated with Christian virgin martyrs.[1] And, in turn, ancient art certainly also demonstrated the brokenness of human existence as well, though this may be an aspect less frequently recalled to mind.

I no longer want to elevate one over the other, to pronounce one the victor and the other the loser to history. Such divisions are the problem, not the solution. The lives of the saints and apostles are far messier than the Christian tradition often allots for, just as Roman ideals were much more difficult to embody than many want to realize.

※

I am continuously baffled by why so few people visit the XII Apostles Church. It is remarkably close to the tourist trail, but it is almost always empty when I visit. Some side chapels, completely open to the public, remain in total darkness for lack of visitors, yet it is an enormous structure with beautiful paintings, especially in the apse, where a cascade of chandeliers drops from the ceiling and points toward one of the more complete and impressive crypts in Rome just under the main altar.

The church as a whole reflects the significance given to the apostles throughout history, since it was their efforts and views that gave life to what was a new religion at the time. It was their willingness to make Jesus' teachings consistent with their own lives, to live out this particular truth and the universality of love that provided the world with a radically new philosophical stance on life.

There is therefore a necessity for the Christian pilgrim to encounter the twelve apostles. I was reminded in fact on this particular occasion of Tom Bissell's efforts to chronicle his pilgrimages to each of the twelve tombs

---

1. Taylor, Rinne, and Kostof, *Rome*, 176.

of the apostles throughout the world—a sign of just how important these encounters may be still for those searching for the presence of Christ.[2]

Preserving the memories of "the Twelve" is in fact akin to the busts of the philosophers, poets, and playwrights of ancient Greece and Rome, as the Capitoline museum maintains in its "hall of philosophers" right next to the "hall of emperors." Though some religious persons might balk at the comparison, equating Greek philosophy with Christian teachings has been done for centuries despite the frequent theological lament that Athens has nothing to do with Jerusalem.

༄

A bunch of contemporary philosophers, however, have sought to bridge this apparent gap and to claim that the uniqueness of Christianity actually resides in its philosophical claims and not simply in its religious, supernatural ones. I am of the opinion that this is the correct reading and recovery of Christianity's truth—and it is a truth still very much in need of hearing again and again.

When Paul writes in his letters that one must let one's identity die— even one's religious, social, or gendered identity—because that is the only way to truly embrace a universal position beyond the particularities of an identity that had been foisted upon us—even the least religious among us cannot ignore the deep truth that still resonates in these claims. To locate our true strength within our apparent vulnerability, which is revealed when we confess that we are not able to identify fully with the identities that have been given to us, is a radical proposition that humanity is still trying to get its head around.

Though it may sound shocking that a nonbeliever might find great merit in some of the core tenets of a particular religious faith, it should not surprise anyone for much longer. Living in a pluralistic age means being willing to access and uplift truth no matter where it is found.

Perhaps *the* sign of maturity and growth in the age in which we live will be our ability to recognize diverse truths *wherever* they may lie, and to embrace them with the vigor we once preserved for religious doctrine, though with a flexibility that signals a new dawn has broken upon us.

---

2. Bissell, *Apostle*.

Listening for Presence

At the MACRO museum, he listens to experimental music—The only spiritual encounter with music that he has in Rome—He draws a parallel between his experiences and sitting in eucharistic adoration in Saint Louis, Missouri

IT WASN'T UNTIL I sat down for a moment in a mostly darkened room in MACRO, Rome's contemporary art museum, to listen to some new, experimental music that I realized, not only how derivative of meditative religious music this specific piece was, but also how, in all my trips to multiple churches over the past week, this was the only spiritual encounter with music that I had.[1]

Though the experience of listening to it felt somewhat disembodied to me—since no community had gathered to listen to the music in that sterile museum space I could simply exit at will—there was a stark, sparse beauty in what I heard. It was clearly an echo of monastic choirs and church organs that infiltrated the otherwise muted atmosphere.

I kept asking myself, as I sat in the tiny, dark space, who this music was for, what community it would speak to, who would gather in a crowd to hear its refrains played over and over again?

So much in this museum accurately reflects trends in contemporary art. What one exhibit labeled as "erratic" could also be labeled as fragmented, surreal, in the form of collage or bricolage, or as genuinely reflecting the breakdown of traditional, canonical forms. I often think of the increased modern frequency of placing tattoos on the body as a cultural sign of this trend: a way of recreating the permanent look of what is naturally given and seemingly beyond our control.

---

1. The music in particular was an electronic piece by Senni, titled "Presto?! Four Musical Procedures" from 10/02 to 12/06/2022.

Though many today stare in bafflement and bemusement at much of contemporary art, I find that it is often the only place where artists are not only pushing back effectively against established meaning and the many ideologies that saturate our world, but it is also a refuge of possibility for new meaning, what we might call the entrance of the sacred by other means.

It is indeed the hallmark of sacrality to recreate all that came before it and to present new opportunities for meaning to occur.

The reading of a poem that brings a new perspective to language often feels sacred for this reason. A work of art that unsettles us and points toward new symbolic vistas contains something of the sacred. A new scientific insight that changes the way we see nature, our world, or ourselves often rushes forth like a holy epiphany or a flash of transcendence, leaving wonder and amazement in its wake. Even the way a natural landscape can deconstruct our narrow worlds with its expansive, dispossessing force brings forth a certain sacredness into our lives.

༄

Museum experiences feel disembodied because they isolate and speak to a part of the human experience that used to be connected to so many other facets of life through monolithic religious sensibilities that had once sought to unite everything. Religion indeed excels at unifying the disparate parts of existence and providing a cohesive symbolic network to tie it all together.

Now that we live in much more fragmented ways, engaging life in piecemeal fashion, often alone or with diverse, unique, and contingent communities, experiences like art can seem so detached from other aspects of our life. But this detachment is deceptive, for it is not total, and new opportunities to identify ourselves and our relations with those around us arise from our fragmented lives in ways we are still trying to comprehend. Such art still has a tremendous power to transform lives and to interact with parts of society and culture, politics and religion, in order to constantly transform our world anew.

༄

Sitting in MACRO listening to the music slowly and steadily pouring meditatively into a small room had reminded me of the feelings I have sometimes had in the past sitting quietly and alone for adoration in a Carmelite monastery in Saint Louis, Missouri. There was an unmistakable resonance between these two moments in time, and I was struck by just how parallel my experiences were.

Adoration has always been one of my favorite Catholic practices. Just a brief moment, or perhaps a long duration, in silence in front of the presence of Christ. Typically, a monstrance on the altar with the exposed, consecrated eucharistic host on display.

Because I had searched for such practices in Rome for years, but had never found a church actively engaging in adoration, I was therefore intrigued at my discovery of a church dedicated to adoration in the midst of sirens, noise, and traffic: S. Claudio, a sanctuary for adoration in the heart of Rome, founded by a Parisian priest.

A brief conversation with a priest there revealed that it was indeed a very uncommon occurrence in Rome to open the church's doors for adoration to all who might wander in from off of one of the main shopping streets in the city.

After our talk, I was left wondering how much more effective the Church's mission might be if more churches practiced this very same thing. Perhaps converting some of the churches from museums back into functional holy spaces would depend on such efforts being consciously undertaken.

The Catholic Church has tried for centuries to appeal to the waning faith of its members and to demonstrate to the general populace that its relevance has not diminished over time. Providing deep glimpses into its traditions and history, its practices and philosophy, may inspire many to retain their commitments to family and institution, and such things may also inspire those outside the Church to take more seriously how it continues to speak to the complexity of particular human experiences, even when it remains willfully unaware of others.

The Layers of History

Stemming the tide of religious decline by turning to the ground beneath the Church—Exploring underneath San Clemente—He finds a humbler version of Christian worship—S. Nicola Encarcere revealing Christianity's tendency to dominate historically over formerly pagan sites—To love the complexity of living in a world haunted by other presences

THERE IS A DENSITY of experience in Rome that I find in few other places. History, for example, is condensed here in a way that never fails to impact one's view of their own personal story. It is impossible not to think about the entirety of one's life—accomplishments, failures, loves, and losses, experiences of both sacredness and the detritus of the streets—when walking through the city and allowing it to overcome you, inviting it to take root in your subconscious and to grow as large as you will let it.

Being open to this density and its unconscious dimensions is essential for the pilgrim, whose body becomes the tuning fork that resonates with the varied layers of experience present in the landmarks that rise up to greet you as you walk slowly through personal and communal histories.

ஐ

The layers of history peel back significantly as I walk in the shadow of the Colosseum, along the road toward the Basilica of San Giovanni in Laterano, and then turn left and duck into the side door of San Clemente.

I first entered the church the way it should be discovered: in a youthful state, completely unaware of the treasures beneath it, but going there trusting the advice of others. The relatively banal artifice of the inner sanctuary, with its unique monastic choir before the altar and its mosaics in the apse

The Layers of History

did not prepare me for the descent I was eventually to make down into the bowels of the church.

It has always been an anachronism to see Peter and Paul wearing Roman senatorial togas, as if they held prominent political positions in ancient Rome, but this is the image we are imparted with while glancing upward at the mosaic work above the main altar at San Clemente.

The central icon of Christ Pantokrator, more commonly found in the Eastern churches, is here a sign of Christ "all powerful," the stern judge who brings his rulings to bear on all of humanity. Eventual theological formulations of God's sovereignty were predicated on political definitions of power, though, to be fair, there really was little distinction between divine and monarchical sovereignty—though theologians would emphasize a major gulf between them. They were essentially the same thing, guaranteeing the monarch's power through the overlapping positions each took.

Centuries after this confusion was abandoned, we still struggle to disentangle their roles, often taking the one for the other and searching to sustain secular glory through entirely human means.

※

It generally goes unnoticed how modern notions of sovereignty, based on nation-states and their justifications of themselves, are derived wholesale from papal decrees regarding the unlimited power of the pope. At those points in history when the pope felt mostly powerless, such as during the pontificate of Pius IX in the mid-nineteenth century, it became imperative for popes to assert their power more than ever.

Pius IX, having lost the Papal States due to Italian unification, suddenly found it necessary to declare the doctrine of papal infallibility. It is not a coincidence of course that the loss of political power for the papacy—which included his being essentially a "prisoner" within the Vatican's walls up until his death—coincided with his supreme assertion of tremendous spiritual powers.[1]

Like so many other parts of Rome, the Catholic Church had felt the critical, rational sting of modernity as a lasting, if at times subtle, blow against faith. It was not just the French Revolution that scared the church

---

1. Taylor, Rinne, and Kostof, *Rome*, 316.

to its core; it was also the slow erosion of tradition at the hands of the critiques of reason, including scientific and technological advancements, that threatened to render the church's long-standing prominence in Europe shockingly marginal.

In an effort to stem the tide of religious decline, many of the churches of Rome turned in the nineteenth century to the ground beneath them, looking for archaeology to justify in the present day what they feared they could not. San Clemente is one of those churches. It stood for centuries over another fourth-century basilica underneath it and began to investigate its own history in an either conscious or unconscious attempt to legitimate itself in a modern context under threat.

What the church discovered, however, was not just a direct link to its own past, but a link to a past it could not entirely conceive of.

Such gestures of powerlessness and the attempted recoveries of influence were on my mind as I paid a modest fee to explore the basilica underneath San Clemente, finding a humbler version of Christian worship speaking far louder than what I often hear above ground in the Church today.

☙

Almost immediately as I went down the stairs, I was entranced by the simplicity of low ceilings, the way in which the lack of artwork and the absence of pageantry brought forth a renewed context for encountering the sacred. Like that of many monastic traditions and Protestant Reformers, the spirituality that appeared before me was sparser, clearer, and cleaner, shorn of aesthetic distractions and offered to whomever might stumble across it.

Surely this had not been the intentions of the Dominicans who ran the church and who had dug beneath it to locate signs of life within the past that justified their present, but the effect was unmistakably similar to what reformers centuries before had sought as well. Somewhere between the levels, a piece of Christian identity was being undone, and without any recognition that this was a substantial consequence of the quest to legitimate the Catholic Church's power in real time.

The force of this power was only heightened upon my seeing the tomb of St. Cyril, missionary to the Slavic peoples, and originator, along with his brother Methodius, of their alphabet. His tomb had been a favorite site for the prayers of Pope John Paul II, who made it a point to pray here during the Cold War as part of his efforts to battle the "godless Communism" he feared would spread farther throughout the globe if left unchecked.

~

Just past St. Cyril's tomb, however, was a series of stairs taking me to a third level, one beneath *both* basilicas. Here, an ancient Roman street ran between buildings now joined to one another, over a stream still flowing beneath them, and straight toward an altar of the Mithraic cult that once occupied this spot prior to Christianity's arrival on the religious scene of ancient Rome.

It is no coincidence that the three altars all align on the same vertical axis, one over another, in a line pointing directly to the heavens. It was a declaration made in order to assert the superiority of Christianity, while also indicating perhaps a subtle respect for the air of sacrality that had preceded it. Though virtually nothing of this ancient Roman cult, a favorite for soldiers, remains since they produced no scripture and guarded their faith in secrecy, something of its ethos has been preserved through the alignment of altars and the preservation of its space.

~

But at this point, questions that sought to counter the Catholic Church's aggressive archaeological bids began to open up my thought a bit wider: Did the church unintentionally open itself to foreign, and potentially subversive elements, by digging too deeply into its own past? Would not the same thing happen to any individual doing the same thing to themselves psychologically, peering deeper into their subconscious? What faith was one to find here, in this particular space given over to competing religious traditions?

Having been raised as a Protestant, and having becoming a convert to Catholicism in my youth, but since having dug deep within and having loosened my religious faith, eventually subverting it altogether, I felt undone by this celebration of history and of its power to undo us all.

What was once hidden had been revealed. What was once taken for granted had been reconceived, just as what I had assumed myself to be was reopened for inquiry. Perhaps these remarks cause concern for those who might feel their faith threatened by an account of how mine was lost. From where I stand, however, if my experiences are not the basis of what pilgrimage is about—being at peace to wander through the ambiguity of life in order to arrive at unexpected destinations and find something wholly beyond what could have been anticipated—I do not know what else should be. This existential uncertainty is the basis for an encounter with the sacred, no matter by what name we call it.

※

S. Nicola Encarcere contains another attempt by the Catholic Church to unearth what lies beneath it, in this case three temples dedicated to the Roman gods Juno, Spes (or "hope"), and Janus, the two-faced god. It is nearly impossible for the layperson to detect the traces of these temples or of any Roman religious presence, though a brief tour of the archaeological dig underneath the church, beginning in the crypt under the main altar, is enough to confirm these overlapping presences in the same location.

This is what is there to be felt: that competing religious traditions haunt one another on these grounds and that neither fully dominates the other. To be haunted is precisely to cede one's possession of a particular place, to admit that one is not alone, certainly not autonomous, and that one can never be wholly detached from what has come before them.

In truth, this is the reality of living anywhere on this planet, where history delves deep (even if we do not recognize it or understand it), and where ecosystems are more often disrupted by human presences that frequently choose to ignore the other living presences all around them.

※

With all of this in mind, I realized that this complexity of living in a world haunted by other presences is precisely why I love Rome.

When I walk through a crypt, tour a catacomb, or find myself at night among dark ruins, I do not feel the slightest fear. Rather, there is a tremendous peace to be received from spaces that consciously recognize their ghosts and their dead, that acknowledge how we all live among such presences and that we must include them in nearly everything else that

The Layers of History

exists. Even Rome's main train station, Termini, is surrounded by museums dedicated to the dead who lie all around the busiest portions of the city.

Every so often while walking along the sidewalk, I come across the gold plaques sunk into asphalt and stone, reminding everyone who passes and notices that there were Jews who once lived here before their arrest, deportation, and murder in Nazi death camps. These golden tablets are placed just outside their former residences, commemorating stark and tragic absences, while also reminding us of the ghosts that not only haunt, but are welcomed to haunt this city and its homes.

As I write these words at a restaurant table in the Jewish quarter of the city, I cannot help but recognize other, more personal layers of history and its ghosts: here was the restaurant that my then wife and I loved to dine at; over there was where we took her sister to eat; along this stretch of the Tiber was where I laughed with my parents as we walked together one night; in this piazza was where my small son had run around kicking a soccer ball, playing with some Roman boys his age.

It is not sentimentality that draws me to replay each scene before my mind's eye, but the sheer fact of their existence within my life's timeline. Each memory invokes a different feeling, from loss and sadness to joy and wonder. Each quickly dissipates in order for another to reformulate and assert itself.

I have an abundance of memories from all my travels here over the past twenty years and I do not always know how to hold them all at the same time in my heart. So I do not sort them at all, and instead let them lie beside one another like the columns, rocks, and tiles that dot the short grasses in the Forum.

Life Suspended

He recalls the destabilizing effects of his divorce—For him, the only path worthy for a pilgrim is the permanent interruption of life—He inhabits a secular perspective that nonetheless longs for a sacred encounter—He defines pilgrimage as a willingness to embrace a new life through a physical displacement that reflects the interior dislocation one already feels

To be a pilgrim means learning to recognize, and trying to embody, the suspension of a life lived normally. The pilgrim traverses the edges of reality and frequently veers off into the undisclosed terrain of human existence, a space so liminal that one might mistake it for that which is not human at all.

In this sense, the pilgrim and the mystic are siblings on the same journey, one embracing the inner world through their external encounters, the other plunging deeper within an often solitary experience of the self to lose all sense of the external. Both, however, find the suspension of their selves to be the path toward the illumination they seek.

It is not just a letting go of the ordinary and the everyday that suffices in such experiences. Such journeys require a more abrupt point of departure. There must be an acknowledgment that the identity that has been formed in this life has been irrevocably canceled, while it has also not departed from us altogether. It has rather been suspended, hollowed out, without the force that it once seemed to command.

One would be tempted to feel less certain, less secure, if the pilgrim still cared about such things.

Life Suspended

The sense of self that one was accustomed to carrying no longer defines who one is when they are a pilgrim; they carry it loosely on their skin like a garment that can be changed, as Kierkegaard once put it.[1] There is in fact nothing in this world that the pilgrim could cling to, could take for themselves, that would entice them.

Everything is jettisoned so that the pilgrimage might be made, so that one's baggage might be that much lighter, and one's ability to carry whatever they find that much more possible.

If there were some way to carry it all with you on the journey, one's possessions, one's identity, one's past, one's sins, one's inclinations, one's status, one's relations—then the pilgrimage would effectively be over, or possibly would never have begun. The permanent interruption of life that is the pilgrim's path, and their *worth* as a pilgrim, is the only path forward, the only path worthy of being taken.

The pilgrim's path is the one that we are all asked to take during certain seasons within our lifetime, and it is one that we have to respond to, whether we want to or not.

After my divorce some years ago I felt detached from my own memories. It was as if the many years of my marriage were someone else's memories, not the recollections and stories that grounded me in my own life. It felt as if I drifted along in the flotsam of events that transpired all around me, and I struggled to feel a part of them. My past became a disembodied reality that I longed to be connected to, but which felt forever out of my reach. I lived in a liminal state, in exile from my own story, compelled to search endlessly for a connection to myself and my past.

I was particularly drawn to material reminders of the past: photographs, old items of clothing, and particular foods. Yet no physical reminder was greater than those geographical locations we had visited together, as the family that we once were: the foreign cities we had traveled to together became the ultimate experience of my dislocation, with each return to any one of them invoking a sense of vertigo. Paris, Brussels, London, San Francisco, Edinburgh, Barcelona, Rome—each city was a cornucopia of smells, tastes, sights, and memories that ceaselessly unfurled more disorientation

---

1. Kierkegaard, *Works of Love*, 88.

within me, but also somehow gestured *to* me as the only way I might possibly unite myself to my own life and its past.

I was continuously called to face something in my past and in myself that I didn't want to confront, that I didn't know how to absorb.

⁂

Pilgrimage speaks to me of a return to something within us that calls us to reunite with our own lives as seen from a space outside of ourselves. We journey as pilgrims beyond ourselves, beyond the ordinary habits of our lives, in order to return to our lives and to grasp them in ways previously unfamiliar to us. A new perspective on our lives, our pasts, our relationships, our failures, and our despair, can only be achieved by entering into—indeed welcoming—a dislocation *from* our lives.

Such a shattering or disorientation, as so many spiritual writers have illustrated over the years, is how faith arrives in our lives as a feeling of coming home to oneself, but only after it first dislocates us from everything we had previously known about ourselves. We are shattered so that we might locate a wholeness, a love even, that transcends whatever we could construct on our own.[2]

It makes an intuitive sense then why those who have lost their jobs, their loved ones, their homes or whatever stability they had previously regarded as foundational in their lives, suddenly feel the need to make a journey to lands otherwise unknown to them order to search for something—something sacred, something perceived as missing but sought after, something deep within themselves, something transcendent—that promises to point the way toward wholeness, healing, peace, and equilibrium. Even if no such wholeness will ever be found, the desire to set out on a search defines us in ways we rarely fathom.

⁂

I enter the churches of Rome feeling detached from the sacred aura that centuries of belief have tried to invest within these walls. I inhabit a secular point of view that nonetheless longs for the sacred encounter, all too aware

---

2. I explore these particular themes more in-depth in my *Theology as Autobiography*.

that such encounters can and do take place every day without a so-called divine being felt as present within one's life.

I have no problem with considering the secular as being the flipside of the sacred, still somehow concealing it within itself, unable to fully eradicate it. Yet this does not mean that I believe in God, either in secret or against myself.

The longing for a sacred encounter will never leave me and I embrace this longing as many things at once: a desire for love, as a never-ending quest for wholeness, as a yearning for connection and relationship that grounds us within our own lives and that makes us feel at home with ourselves, if only for a short while.

I do not seek out God when I enter a church in Rome, though I believe I do seek what the saints had also once sought for themselves: to battle my sense of failure, yet to consider my weaknesses as the only path toward strength, to find my vulnerability as a greater exposure to life itself, to deconstruct my desires in order to find an eventual wholeness, to repel the desire to find all the answers, to submit to forces larger than myself, to lay down my burdens, to stand outside of my life and to gain new perspectives by doing so, to heal old wounds, to find the strength to keep going in the face of despair and hopelessness, to be exposed to grace, to find redemption for what I had felt to be lost, to rest from my struggles, to harbor more peace than strife, and to sit in the silence until I hear a still small voice speaking directly to me, giving my life back to me in a form I had never seen it in before. Perhaps some would call such encounters sacred—I know I do.

I don't want to undo the paradoxes that are littered throughout my life, the tensions between the sacred and the profane that I reside in, locatable somewhere between belief and unbelief. I want to sit in paradox and mystery unresolved, making peace with their existence until I am also at peace with my own paradoxes and mysteries.

There is no autonomously existing sacredness to anything on this earth—things are sacred because they exist in a significant web of relations that are impossible to comprehend fully. Histories, objects, persons, and places all converge to provide a "charge" of the sacred to a particular nexus of relations. These spaces where so many people have gathered to offer their prayers, where hope has been cultivated within the heat of despair, and where many have searched for a relationship foundational to their sense of life, somehow become places where we can open ourselves up to something beyond ourselves.

Though perhaps not as many might imagine the sacred to be, such sites offer us a glimpse into our own humanity and open us up to a radically foreign otherness that yet characterizes who we are, and are not, to ourselves.

༄

It makes sense that many mystics and saints have found that facing their own personal depths was akin to dying to themselves. Death is often feared or ignored, rarely faced or accepted. The entire Christian story points to little more than a willingness to face one's own death and the ordinariness of those "miracles" we find in the new life given to us when we come through a symbolic death to the other side of things.

Churches are monuments to this desire to let go of one's life and to seek one's reward in darkness, not knowing if there is anything truly valuable on the far end of what we can see. It is like sailing into a dense fog without any guidance or assurance of safety as we enter into the density of it all.

༄

The loss of my religious faith has certainly felt like a death at times, one that accompanied the loss of my marriage and has not left me since. My grief is palpable and ever present, and I can't shake the feeling that I am being asked to give up more still. It is not God or the universe that calls me to do this. It is my own awareness that the fullness of my own humanity—if I am to find more maturity, more wisdom—begs me to let go of everything I had thought mattered and that seemed essential to my sense of self, purpose, and worth.

Each step I take toward the next "sacred space" is another step further away from the ghosts of my own desires and dreams that had fueled my sense of who I was, and was wanting to be, for decades. I am not sure how I will find a way to exist or cope beyond the life I have known, but I know I must die to that life and be born into something else entirely.

How many missionaries or devout faithful have already descended along this same path? Any worthy of their faith, no doubt.

It feels somewhat ironic that I share in this quest with them yet without their God. Even though their path feels familiar, perhaps is even the very same one.

※

On the street near the Franciscan university in Rome, the Antonianum, I notice an icon of Mary affixed to a wall along the edge of the sidewalk. Those casually passing by are invited to enter into this common space through the image of holiness that reaches out to greet them with a sudden disorientation typically experienced in confrontations with poverty or mental illness on the street.

So many simple shrines and religious iconography adorn the many busy routes of Rome one may traverse day by day, some in tiny alcoves in the side of homes, as in more traditional segments of Catholic Europe throughout the centuries.

When I lived in Belgium, for example, there were many such spaces, a majority of which were empty, reflecting the rapidly changing landscape of a modern, secular society. Even the empty placeholder, however, can be a source of inspiration to pause and turn inward in order to assess the daily state of one's interior life. A reminder too that even what appears to be gone can point to a significant reality still deep within.

The proliferation of those memorial sites to the deceased along roadways can function as a *memento mori*, a reminder of our mortality, that which has for centuries helped humans to comprehend what, in the short lives we live, ultimately matters and what does not.

※

I have said multiple times over the past several years—and deeply meant it—that if it were possible at this point in time to walk away from my life and take up something new, I would. The obvious love for my son, the stability of a job I actually enjoy, and many other smaller factors prevent this suggestion from unfolding into a lived reality—thankfully. But such sentiments are nonetheless true to my feelings and a reminder of how struggle can accompany me anywhere, at any time.

A friend of mine, whose divorce coincided with her children's independence and the desire to switch careers, did just this: walked away from it all and moved across the country in pursuit of the solitude of nature and a lifestyle that more directly suited her.

I was envious of her boldness, envious of her ability to leave everything else behind. Her previous life had died and it was fitting to see her embrace its symbolic fulfillment through the uprooting of nearly everything else in her orbit.

Pilgrimage is just this: a willingness to embrace a new life through a physical displacement that reflects the interior dislocation one already feels. It is not the most appealing state to be in when one actually lives such a reality on a daily basis, but it is an accurate portrayal nonetheless, one that needs to be acknowledged for what it is and fully embraced in order to understand what it is that the pilgrim must become.

Beyond the Walls

He enters San Lorenzo fuori le mura—He recalls a personal triangulation: the end of his marriage, his broken foot, and a loss of faith—He feels disconnected from his former selves, yet also feels peace—He reflects on the tactics that Pope Pius IX used to save the church from modernity and concludes that a future is possible—For him, both tradition and openness are needed for the Church's future—Knowing with certainty that his faith is gone, he finds himself more compelled than ever to go back inside the churches of Rome

THERE ARE A NUMBER of prominent churches in Rome that lie "fuori le mura" or "outside the walls" of the city proper. It is to the smaller ones among them that I am often drawn, as they offer a solitude and a solace that frequently cannot be found within the city's walls.

For a variety of reasons, San Lorenzo "fuori le mura" is the one that I favor, and I found myself entering its nave on a cool summer morning at a time when no one else had chosen to partake in its silences.

The quietness that resides between the stones of the structure became a space in which I wanted to dwell, if only for a moment.

The unusual interior structure was intriguing to me, for it is as if two distinct building projects that nonetheless differed little in style were joined in the center, two separate churches promising a capacity to bring together things that had once been torn asunder. When the interior form matches the awkwardness of the silence without abandoning it, I feel the potential for peace to radiate outwards and inwards alike.

The sparsity of the sanctuary is complemented by the expansiveness of the choir, with its arched balconies and mosaic-work reserved for those who dare to walk beyond the altar. Though the *confessio* would eventually beckon me to walk beneath the main floor, I took a moment to compose myself before continuing on to what ultimately drew me there.

Sacred Pilgrim, Secular Pilgrim

It is painful to me even now to recall the triangulation of forces that pinned me to a chair in that particular church on that particular morning: the need for solitude as my marriage was ending, the pain of a broken right foot sustained while playing basketball in Brazil the week before, and the realization that I had not believed in God in many years. All of these things bore a tremendous weight that I found harder and harder to carry.

Or at least, this is what I had expected myself to feel—a sort of unending pulse that would not detach itself from me.

The truth, however, was something I discovered that summer.

I was not burdened by these three things at all: I was actually liberated by them, though I could not always see this reality so clearly. Though my grief was very real, the dissolution of my marriage also brought about a certain happiness through the ending of a shared suffering. There was a freedom in this experience in particular that I had not felt in years, if ever, and I had no desire in that moment to rush headlong into a foolish compensatory relationship. I was content simply to sit in the absence of a presence, in the silence that echoed off nearly everything I saw or touched.

The broken foot was manageable, though undiagnosed and deeply difficult to walk on. The fact that I had not yet sought proper medical treatment didn't help matters. What I soon found to be true was that having a broken foot actually forced me to venture out only when it felt absolutely necessary, not to take any extraneous steps but to restrict myself in ways that focused me, sharpened my senses, and made me more aware of my surroundings.

Lastly, despite the recognition that religion and God no longer played the role they once did in my life, there were still new roles for them to play. The thought actually stirred me, brought me to San Lorenzo fuori le mura, as I too nestled under its umbrella trees, and caused me to search for different presences in my life, like the occasional companions—colleagues and students from a course I taught at that time—who would take the time to walk through Rome with me in my troubled though often concealed state.

I felt disconnected, dislocated from my former life, from each of my former selves, but there was also a peace that ran throughout my entire body, and which I carried into the empty church that morning.

I am certain too that I carried a slightly different peace out with me as a result of my being there.

※

I remember spending so much time in Rome by myself, right before the separation, laying around with a broken foot and needing to rest it a lot, the feeling that I was squandering my time by laying around but well aware that I could do nothing more than rest.

I first came to Rome on my honeymoon more than twenty years ago and I remember how my senses were yearning to come alive. The smells, tastes, and sights in particular were all a source of endless fascination and wonder. Touching the cold marble was almost obligatory everywhere I went and I would listen to the sounds of the city as if I had never heard such noises before.

I recall too how all of my senses seemed dulled the summer of my separation, muted by the recognized end of my marriage. Various wines and an abundance of chocolate became little more than numbing agents, as my desire to seek out new experiences there was almost nonexistent, which is a terrible thing to feel when in such a beautiful place.

Though that summer was many years ago now, I am still living somewhat under its spell, wishing I could sense and feel more than I do, but knowing that I also can't simply force myself to be open before I am ready.

The missing piece is, and has always been, love, and I struggle to give it at times because I was hurt by being denied it.

※

It is exceedingly hard, if not impossible, to feel part of a relationship that was not destined to last for as long as it was supposed to. I believe this to be the case because we are unable to express the complexity and mystery of who we are to ourselves. It is easier to find confirmation and resonance with who we are in the reflection of another and in an intimacy that can be shared.

Bringing the intricacies and nuances of who we are into alignment with another human being leaves us feeling as if the combination of two inexpressible individuals had to be guided, or at least more fully understood, by forces well beyond our limited comprehension.

I thought of this when I walked into a nondescript Roman church today and felt the resonance between the desires for transcendence bound up with an old Roman missal and my own desires to be caught up in the complexity of religious faith. Catholicism has sought for millennia to conjoin the various facets of our lives into a deep, rich, symbolic universe, one that makes sense of the confusions of both our words and ourselves.

To belong to an organized, religious faith is to let go of some of the confusion, though not all of it, that belabors human existence—to let go of one's distrust and anxiety at not knowing how so much of oneself fits together. The beautiful, rational, and critical faculties of our minds rightly point out those traditions, beliefs, and institutions we should be skeptical about. But, in truth, we also cannot live in a heightened state of critique and mistrust for a prolonged period of time. We have to find ways to embrace and be passionate about our relationships with others.

The desire to want to believe and to trust is a wholly good one and one that needs to be affirmed and cultivated properly, despite the fact that it can also be easily abused, as many a political ideology or distorted religious fundamentalism can attest to. The fullness of our humanity and a respect for its complexity will only be witnessed by embracing those traits for belonging and letting go that religious traditions have spent centuries helping others to achieve. Despite our modern propensity to be hypercritical of religious doctrinal claims that often strain our credulity, we have to locate sound practices that further acquaint us with our desires to belong and also to let go, to believe and to resonate.

൪

As the German philosopher Martin Heidegger once remarked toward the end of his own deeply troubled life, there is something special about those sacred sites where humans have gathered for centuries to grieve, to pray, to offer up their sacrifices, to engage the deepest recesses of their humanity in order to find something beyond themselves.

Such raw vulnerability cannot fail to move those who are able to sense its presence among them.

I felt honored to be in this place, at this moment in my life, to be open to my own story and the goodness still and forever present within it. I was open to the mysteries of the sacred before me, even as I had left some of them behind.

The complicated nature of my own life was nothing new to the Church, where martyrs lay beside deeply complex leaders who offered no uncomplicated narratives of their time spent on this earth. The fact that the church of San Lorenzo had been largely destroyed during an American bombing run in the Second World War seemed symbolically fitting, more than appropriate for my circumstances that cool summer morning.

☙

The complexity and weight faded a bit in the light as I found myself drifting toward the back of the church, past the tombs of Saints Lawrence and Stephen in the *confessio*, to the final resting place of a pope who has no easy historical determination for us today.

Pius IX was a fierce resister of modernity—often, it seemed, of change itself. He was frequently bent on preserving his power at a time when such tactics were reminiscent of former glories of the papacy and little more. He feared the waning influence he had would soon be taken from him entirely, so he began to shift power from its political moorings to its social exchange. He issued global calls for solidarity among Catholics "beyond the mountains" (*ultramontane*) that divided nation-states alongside a proliferation of pictures of himself as *the* unifying image of one's Catholic devotion.

He set the course of Catholicism in the modern age by resisting cultural changes and crying foul when someone attacked his "right to religious freedom," such as when he legitimated the kidnapping of a small Jewish boy whom, he claimed, had been secretly baptized by a Catholic servant girl who feared that the boy might suddenly die from a particularly severe, but nonetheless temporary, illness. It was a scandal at the time, especially to the Jewish community in Italy, but nonetheless a reflection too of unjust laws, anti-Semitic views within the church, and a general sense of cultural superiority amongst Catholics in Italy.[1]

☙

I walked directly to the tomb placed in the farthest corner of the church, a partial crypt existing in the shadows as if it were ashamed of itself, yet also far too lavishly constructed for a church dedicated to simpler, early martyrs of the Church.

---

1. Kertzer, *Kidnapping of Edgardo Mortara*.

Sacred Pilgrim, Secular Pilgrim

It was more than ironic that, in the midst of my own loss of faith, I had made a pilgrimage to the tomb of a pope dedicated to resisting the forces of secularism in Europe and the world. But there was something that attracted me in this story, something I admired in the complexity of his life that I would most likely have not admired in the man himself should we have ever had the chance to meet.

How is one to face the rapid changes of modern culture when so firmly rooted in such old and storied traditions? This is not an easy question to answer and an even more difficult one to live.

Resisting the advances of biblical scholarship, aligning oneself with monarchs and dictators while denouncing democracy, ignoring reason while championing the sacred heart—these were the religious tactics of a Church living in fear. The terrors of the French Revolution were still in the air throughout the reign of Pius IX, and the Catholic Church had reason to fear that its centuries of tradition might soon be ignored, or even dissolved, as had happened already in France.

The Italian general Giuseppe Garibaldi and the cause of Italian unification was soon to take away the Papal States from among the pope's possessions, thereby legitimating Pius's fears. In a way that parallels Catholic zeal, it is even possible to imagine Garibaldi's military journey as a leader of Italian unification as a pilgrimage in its own right, as Tim Parks has done.[2]

Criticisms of religion were more vocal, public, substantial, and influential than ever before. It is hardly surprising that the Church began to embody a "siege mentality," becoming more inward looking and insular, a trend that has not always abated with time, despite the Church's attempts to modernize itself such as with the Second Vatican Council in the mid-twentieth century.

Pius IX's story, to my ears, is a sad one of missed opportunities and a conscious fostering of unnecessary oppositions, leading to a variety of repressions. It is a cautionary tale for those who do not listen to what others speak

2. Parks, *Hero's Way*.

truth about, and who therefore remain unwilling to change in the face of major cultural shifts taking place all around them.

Though I may disagree with the Catholic Church's stance on many issues, I am nonetheless reminded *by* the church that taking a stand for tradition and community often happens when the erosion of centuries of accumulated wisdom appears to be taking place at an unprecedented rate. From my point of view, religion's decline is obvious and widespread, and a trend that I am not inclined to see being reversed. But, from among the wreckage, there is so much to be used, so much to be rebuilt in new forms we have yet to discover and embrace.

I came to this tomb specifically because it had signaled to me, more than perhaps anywhere else in Rome, that a future *is* possible. It is not the one that Pius IX would have hoped was carried forward, but it is a future of possibility nevertheless—one that comes to light only through efforts such as his to preserve what is most valuable in our religious traditions.

Though his tactics to save the church were mostly temporary, reactionary measures, they tell me that an openness was, and is still, needed—one that goes beyond any defense of a given tradition and looks to embrace what unites us as human beings.

᷾

Though this sentiment will perhaps strike some religious persons as a naïve universalism or a blind humanistic urge, I disagree. There will always be a need for tradition and community, and no certain way to defend one's particular tradition or community over any other's existence. In an age of pluralization, we must become open to the differences and let them in, allow them to change us entirely, and then we can go back into the specific traditions that have been so meaningful to humankind throughout the centuries.

The recovery will only happen once we allow ourselves to be taken apart and put back together again anew—as I had been learning very intimately in my own life on that occasion.

Ironically, then, it was only after losing my faith and knowing with certainty that it was gone that I found myself open to something like a new type of faith. It was only then that I felt almost compelled to go back into such churches, to become a pilgrim as often as I can allow myself.

Fighting Modernity

He offers two examples of churches, Sacre Coeur basilica and Basilica del Sacro Cuore di Gesu, working to circumvent the rising currents of modern skepticism toward religious belief—He describes how Pope Pius X's pontificate tried to block the influences of modernity—He admits that such divisions are a distraction for the pilgrim—He also asks himself, as a pilgrim, how to transcend such divisions

IT IS NO COINCIDENCE that the reaction to modern forces of rationality and critique that Pius IX resisted are historically linked to a rise in perceiving faith as an emotional appeal to one's heart. This was a time, after all, when Pope Pius IX declared the immaculate conception (regarding Mary's birth, not Jesus') as an assertion of papal infallibility *and* when a certain anti-Enlightenment devotion to the Sacred Heart of Jesus began to flourish.

The Sacré Coeur basilica in Montmartre, Paris was built during this time, for example, drawing the faithful deeper into an emotive spirituality rather than rational argument.

It was also a time when Marian apparitions began to appear throughout Europe, such as at Lourdes in France, and, sometime afterwards, at Fátima in Portugal. These Marian apparitions were often linked to Ultramontane ideals and to a person's declared loyalty to the papacy, or even just authoritarianism, as many global, Catholic dictators were devout Marianists, such as Francisco Franco in Spain and Augusto Pinochet in Chile.

Pius IX's view was that only Catholics should be free to worship as they pleased and that modernity should be condemned in multiple forms. It was as an attempt to eliminate modern unbelief that the First Vatican Council was called in 1868, where papal infallibility was made a doctrine in the face of a loss of the Papal States, which were being defended in war, but which were ultimately lost by the pope in 1870.

In fact, the first Vatican Council never truly concluded, as King Victor Emmanuel of Italy invaded Rome and took over the Vatican, effectively suspending the council entirely.

In the end, Vatican City was established as its own little kingdom, complete with a post office, bank, and so forth, but its political power was stripped from it almost entirely. As a concession, however, the pope was, at long last, allowed to choose all the bishops over Italy—something that had not been possible before.[1] The pope wouldn't be able to appoint all bishops the world over, however, until a revision of canon law took place under Pope Pius X in 1917.[2] In response to these traumatic events, Pius forbid Catholics from holding political office or from voting in Italian politics at all—a position that effectively stayed in place until shortly after WWI.

꿁

After Pius IX died in 1878—having served the longest pontificate in history up until that point—the church was entirely transformed, leaving a strong conservative, Ultramontane vision in its wake. In one historian's words, "Ultramontanes identified Catholicism with *Romanitas*: they saw the unity of the Church as inextricably tied to uniformity. One faith *meant* one discipline, one liturgy, one code of canon law, one pyramid of authority presided over by a proactive and interventionist papacy."[3]

Pius IX's body was moved to San Lorenzo at night, and there were even large crowds of anti-clerical protestors present seeking to throw his coffin into the Tiber. This was, of course, a time of Italian patriotic sentiment, when many Italians were openly defiant of the Church, even going so far as to erect large statues of Garibaldi throughout the city.

The Catholic Church, for its part, entered a state of siege mentality that sought to block the influence of modernity altogether. An example of such a mentality would be found in the pontificate of Pope Pius X, who followed Pius IX very closely in his agenda, administering an "anti-Modernist Oath" that academics, for example, had to take in order to teach—and which was used until the 1960s.

---

1. Duffy, *Saints and Sinners*, 302.
2. Duffy, *Saints and Sinners*, 322.
3. Duffy, *Saints and Sinners*, 304.

His pontificate also supported orthodox, conservative organizations that spied and reported on alleged modernist movements within the church, engaging in "witch hunts" against those deemed heretics and using a language to identify "real Catholics" in favor of those who compromised the integrity of the Catholic faith. "Obedience, not enquiry, became the badge of Catholic thought," as one historian has put it.[4] With some notable exceptions, one might say that popes have since striven to embody that "mystique of the papacy" that accompanied the doctrine of papal infallibility in order to be the "last absolute monarchs" in the world.[5]

All of this is to say that pilgrimage sites are often contested sites, with multiple forces at play on their grounds at any given moment. To be enthralled at a Marian shrine does not make one a papal loyalist, though it certainly doesn't hurt your chances of becoming one, as one of the bullets from Pope John Paul II's assassination attempt being placed in the crown of Our Lady of Fátima nicely illustrates.

To see the world in a particular way means that one has been persuaded to see it as such by the many experiences and teachings that one has accrued over a lifetime. Different places provoke different reactions in people because they are in very different places in their lives, a reality that can often be hard to see underneath the surface of things.

The Basilica del Sacro Cuore di Gesù, or Sacred Heart of Jesus, located a few steps from the Termini train station in the heart of Rome, is another nineteenth-century testament to Catholicism's attempts to fight the modern tide of unbelief. From the gigantic statue of Pope Pius IX to the appeals of feeling and emotion that the "sacred heart" embodies, to the modern religious iconography and its aching sentimentality, to its overtly evangelistic atmosphere, Sacred Heart tries to stand fast against the rising currents of modern skepticism toward religious belief.

---

4. Duffy, *Saints and Sinners*, 329.
5. Duffy, *Saints and Sinners*, 328–29, 332.

Fighting Modernity

There is a distinct emphasis here on speaking as directly as possible to the demanded relevance of contemporary faith, going so far as to include an empty box with paper beside it and encouraging people to write letters directly to the Virgin Mary.

☙

The ornate and spacious interior is, however, often at odds with these simplistic gestures to reach the average Catholic in the pew. The abundant gold leaf and the image of a Church triumphant, which cascades down from the dome and ceiling on high, sits ill at ease with the fake flowers and plastic statue of Jesus that greets you as you enter the nave.

I do not know if the contemporary Church finds success in making these specific overtures to those it seeks to shepherd. But I do see the icons and images of popular saints taking up more and more room within Roman churches.

The miraculous cross on display at the church of S. Marcello in Corso in Rome has, for example, become a repository for a fair number of pilgrims who come to light candles and pray silently before it. As with so many churches in Rome, this one has sought to brand itself with this particular cross, showcasing pictures of Pope Francis praying before it and luring tourists to stand before it as well. Popular icons of John Paul II, Mother Teresa, and Padre Pio, alongside the Virgin Mary, are scattered throughout the church, appealing to growing Catholic pieties among the devout who find their way here.

☙

It is difficult to know what to feel in such spaces where the tensions embedded within modern Catholicism are impossible to ignore, and where various ongoing "culture wars" that predate, but lay the groundwork for, our own are visible everywhere. How one might transcend such divisions in order to not be overcome by them is a difficult proposition for anyone, and it is a particular distraction for the pilgrim that has to be accounted for at nearly every turn in today's Roman landscape.

Conversion of the Pilgrim

He starts a new day at S. Agostino church and is drawn to Caravaggio's panting Madonna of the Pilgrims—He reflects upon the entanglement of Paul's conversion, bringing Judaic roots into his new life as a Christian—He, following Paul's lead, defines conversion as a change, a process of "turning around" that also entails a translation from one context to another—He visits San Paolo fuori le Mura and reflects upon the legend of Saint Paul's beheading—The modern pilgrim finds a richness in oneself by shutting off the distractions of modern society

S. AGOSTINO, WITH ITS rich colors set in marble and its play of light and shadow throughout the nave, suits the Caravaggio painting there—*Madonna of the Pilgrims*—which sits quietly in a small side chapel just to the left of the main entrance. The kneeling pilgrims show clear signs of weariness and the dirt that accompanies the ardent journeyer. It is as if Caravaggio has anticipated the droves who come year after year to this tiny nook within a grand church in order to rest their gaze on this image.

I began my day here because I felt inexplicably drawn to this painting. Perhaps because it is the opposite of those popular pietistic images I had seen earlier in the day. The weariness caused by my own burdens led me to this space of its own accord, and I had no need to rise too quickly and depart. Whatever popular sentiments sustained the faith of some seemed lost on this visual meditation of the rigor, poverty, and hardship that the pilgrim must take up if they are to encounter a truly holy presence in their lives.

The way the two pilgrims in the painting kneel before Mary is what continuously moves me most in this imaginative depiction, as if the medieval pilgrim were transported back in time and were able to appreciate the vision of grace before them. It is their humanity that speaks directly to me: the dirty bare feet, their age shown through wrinkles, the shabbiness of their clothing, and yet the intense fervor with which they fall to their knees before the object of their adoration.

※

I stare at the image for some time, wondering what it takes to have such visions, to allow oneself to be transported like this to another time, to sit transfixed before a presence long sought after. I would hope that the experience would be utterly transformative, a new sense of dislocation that would, eventually, in turn, ground everything else.

Soon I notice that I am praying, not with words, not necessarily in a religious sense, but not against it either; not lifting my desires to God, but not without God either—merely allowing the deepest core of who I am to escape my bounds and to rise up to wherever it may go. I feel my body praying and I confess my vulnerability and desire for a conversion to take place within my life.

※

Pilgrimage, more traditionally conceived, is about reaching a specific holy site and in this sense has a definite end or conclusion. Just as we seek resolution to life's largest problems, so too do we look to pilgrimage as a journey to be completed at a definitive time and place.

As I have been describing things, however, pilgrimage is also experienced as deeply meaningful even when there is no specific end or goal to which we aspire. It is about being open to change, to a journey we cannot control, to getting lost and admitting that some wandering is good for us.

In truth, pilgrimage is a ceaseless dialectic between these two notions of what it is. It is an unresolvable tension that we must make peace with as we search for answers and yet live within an unending mystery of our own existence.

Our relationship to our bodies—so central to the significance of pilgrimage—runs parallel to this tension, and is even implicated in it, or perhaps is constitutive of it. We can abstract from our embodied state in order to transcend our lived conditions with our bodies: we can fast, swim in ice cold waters, or go without sleep for extreme periods of time. We can entertain thoughts and ideas that need not consider our embodied state. Yet we also have very real bodies with very real needs and desires that have to be accounted for. This is a tension that will never go away and never should.

Pilgrimage expresses this tension within our embodied state by asking us to put our bodies in play within an abstracted, transcendent space—a sacred space to be precise. Pilgrimage brings our bodies into contact with our most transcendent ideas in order to bring some wholeness to our existence, if even for just a moment.

Our bodies are inseparable from our minds, even if our modern life has often tried to separate them.

*

There is a standard definition of conversion that is something like the movement from one religious tradition to another, set within a long history of such journeying as a transition from "error" to "truth," or possibly from "heresy" to "orthodoxy," if these terms are even suitable.

Portraying things as such, however, is a very difficult thing to sustain in this day and age, and is mainly, I think, an unhelpful use of a polarized, and polarizing, logic that is frequently invoked when people talk about doctrine, religious institutions, or the cultures and traditions of a particular religious people.

*

Despite these associations, there is still a truth that lies in this general configuration of reality. Many religious converts do find a new way of living that brings them from a sort of darkness to a sort of light—another polarized logic—and there is no denying the efficacy and power of such a journey.

I do not want to critique or remove such a personal life-affirming transition within someone's story, and I find it difficult to critique such intimate experiences even when they are wrapped in overtly religious-political tones.

At the same time, however, there are those whose manner of framing their journey either falsely romanticizes their conversion or, for others, grants it a certain sacred aura that legitimates a number of newly adopted religious perspectives that appear, for a time at least, to give a person a stable sense of identity.

There is also, I might add, a long history of forced conversions made under the impression that the trajectory from "heresy" to "orthodoxy" was the only movement desirable, though it is best not to replicate these moments in time. There is a sense today that we are better off respecting and leaving alone the divergent cultures and traditions that make up today's globalized network of religions.

It is almost merely good manners, in fact, not to suggest that a Theravada Buddhist from Sri Lanka consider an Americanized version of Presbyterianism as a more proper fit for them, for example. But, then again, there may be some Sri Lankans who feel an inner impulse pushing them toward a certain type of Presbyterianism, though I suspect any form of such a leaning needs to come from deep within the person contemplating their own conversion, and not just from some inbuilt missionary fervor with its own sense of what is "orthodox" and what is "heretical."

☙

Conversion can generally mean a good many things, including a turn from sinfulness to the love of God—whatever this might look like as an embodied religious practice—a change in character, or, simply, the turn to a different object on our horizon.

This would sum things up for many persons, I suspect, but I also doubt matters were this underwhelming for Saint Paul, at the time known as Saul, whose eyes were paradoxically opened by a bright light, though he saw nothing immediately, saw nothing quite literally until the "scales fell from his eyes."[1] Like a good convert, Paul realized much later that, though he had had a tremendous encounter with God, he was not fully formed in his faith, and needed to learn from others what this newfound sense of self within him was to be.

But, we should also note, and as we further learn from his writings, Paul never fully left behind his Judaic roots either. They were very central to the person he remained. It was not entirely clear to the earliest Christians that their "Jesus movement" was anything other than a reform-based initiative *within* the heart of Judaism.

---

1. Acts 9:18.

Paul, at the same time as he embraced his encounter with the "risen Lord," may not have been so eager to leave his Judaism behind, and this despite the fact that he certainly began to expand the sense of what it meant to be a Jew in the first place, opening the doors still wider toward the gentile population he felt could stand for a heavy dose of Jesus' radical teachings.

What Paul was learning, I suspect, was how to translate his roots into a new context, one that also remained within the "old" context (in this case, a Jewish one) as much as anything else.

In fact, I'm not convinced that he ever really disentangled his being-Jewish from his newfound sense of being-Christian at all. The nexus of Judeo-Christian thought is entangled with the processes of conversion itself. This entanglement seems to speak directly to how Christianity grew from Judaism. Perhaps this paradoxical experience can teach us something still.[2]

✍

These things are just some of what I thought about one day when looking at the façade of San Paolo fuori le mura, another church tucked far away from the touristic center of the old city. I too felt caught between traditions, religious and secular, and I found that not separating them completely was a tremendous source of my own identity, as well as its appeal, much as Paul had strained and succeeded in bringing his Judaic roots into his new context as a follower of the Christ.

My definition of conversion, following Paul's lead, is one rooted in the Latin sense of *conversio* (from *converto*), which indicates a process of "turning around," a change or alteration, but which also conveys a sense of a translation taking place, something which implies, to my mind, keeping multiple languages, religions, and traditions alive and "in play" as it were.

---

2. In suggesting that the "entangled" relationship between Judaism and Christianity has a positive lesson to teach us, I am well aware too of the much needed historical argument that this mixture of the Judeo-Christian has also led, at times, to an unfair linkage between the two faiths, one that has mainly benefited Christians while refusing the recognize the legitimate existence of Jews who were often persecuted and consistently oppressed. My remarks are not intended to take that path. The difference between such histories and what I would offer on the contrary is that I would rather point toward the undoing of a singular religious identity from *within*, as a process of self-critique, self-reflection, and confession, and not from *without*, as an external co-optation of one religious identity by another.

What I want to isolate within such a dynamic interplay of identities and communities is the notion that conversion entails a necessary translation from one context to another, which in the end also implicates *both* contexts. Such an idea intrigues me deeply, and gives me some solace too, because I believe it to be true that when you undergo an authentic conversion, whether religious or not, you never really leave behind the place where you came from. Yet, you do translate everything into a new idiom, and hope you are better off for the effort.

ꙮ

As one of the twin pillars of the early church, alongside the apostle Peter, Paul was martyred in Rome in the middle of the first century while pursuing missionary work there, starting up house churches (*domus ecclesia*), and generally spreading the "good news" of the Jesus event.

There is a legend that when Paul was beheaded, his head bounced three times on the ground, pouring milk instead of blood. Each time it struck the ground, a fountain sprung up, hence the cemetery was christened "The Three Fountains." A Benedictine monastery on the grounds there, Le Tre Fontane, founded itself as a memorial to this tale. Though we now know that this site would have been too far away from the city of Rome proper for an execution, legend places it at this site, probably to bolster its authenticity and to cultivate reverence for the location itself.

ꙮ

The first time I saw this immense structure of a church, the image of milk instead of blood reminded me of something I had once read in the writings of the English mystic Julian of Norwich about how "mother Christ" gave birth to the Church on the cross as he died.[3] The separation of blood from water that appeared from his side, to her mind, indicated the birth of a child, when the mother's water breaks before the blood comes forth.

My hunch is that this particular Pauline legend and its pouring of milk from the saint's body is somehow symbolically linked to such a notion—another death that gave birth to the Church as it were.

---

3. Julian of Norwich, *Revelations of Divine Love*.

The church itself wasn't built until the fourth century, during the Roman Emperor Constantine's reign, and it was constructed directly over St. Paul's original burial site, as burials at the time were not allowed within the city walls. Though it has been rebuilt many times throughout the centuries after an earthquake (1349), fires (1115 and 1823, which destroyed much of the interior, leaving a very spacious feeling to it, though the basilica wasn't restored fully until 1930), the sacking of Rome by foreign invaders (739, 773, and 843), and flooding (1700), it is actually the second largest basilica in Rome after the spectacular San Pietro, and was even consecrated on the same day as San Pietro on November 18, 324.

The immensity of the sanctuary easily floods the senses, imposing a sense of almost divine foreboding amidst conscious and unconscious nods to God's sovereignty. As one of the four major basilicas of Rome, San Paolo fuori le Mura is meant to intimidate, but also meant to envelop those who enter it into the deep history of the Church that expands far beyond these fortress-like walls.

Until the twentieth century, the large structure stood alone in the midst of an open field, as there were not many buildings in the area at that time. I like to imagine it standing as a solitary beacon to the wandering pilgrim throughout the years, though this is hard to conceive of today as it stands amidst so many enormous apartment buildings and businesses.

It is hard to comprehend the significance of such a church in the present day where once, when the popes fled to Avignon, France, it was considered as *the* site in Rome for the pope's second in command, especially in the pope's absence from the city.[4]

---

4. The Avignon papacy, or "Babylonian Captivity," was a time when the papal residency relocated to Avignon, France, and Rome fell into decay, from 1309 to 1376, from Popes Clement V to Gregory XI. It was also a time of great warfare for the popes, but also a step away from Roman family feuding and influence. During this time, the Vatican established departments, or congregations, and became more centered on legal structures and systems, not a reliance upon the mystical power of relics (Duffy, *Saints and Sinners*, 166).

Conversion of the Pilgrim

Until the seventeenth century, moreover, when San Pietro was consecrated, this was *the* pilgrimage site that the faithful coming to Rome sought out. It looks remarkably a lot like it did in the fourth century in terms of size as well, which indicates just how impressive it was as an early pilgrimage site. The fact that the tomb of Paul was accessible for the consecration of relics dropped into his tomb made this site even more significant for pilgrims.

As I walked through the opulent courtyard, a breeze moved the trees around the statue of Paul, which holds a sword to indicate the means of his death. I entered the palatial basilica to find only a handful of persons moving about slowly across its marble floor.

Unlike San Pietro, which is a magnet for pilgrims and tourists alike, and nearly inaccessible for meditative moments for that very reason, San Paolo can easily become an oasis for the reflective. It offers the immensity and stature of a larger church alongside an unmatched quietude. Indeed, the only sounds that I heard there that day emanated from the *confessio*, or space just under the main altar, where a modest sized group of Polish pilgrims were singing in hushed tones while gathered around Paul's tomb.

The sheer emptiness of this space, and the silence that results from it, are both palpable and desirable. As someone bereft of organized religious faith, I feel that coming into this unique place offers me the chance to unite two disparate parts of myself, a religious past and a secular present, in the hopes of a future conjunction that might sustain me throughout the years to come.

I was not caught in a tension that I wished to escape. I was intentionally immersing myself further within that tension, probing the limits of myself from within the silence of an almost emptied sacred space. What grandeur and glory this formerly prominent pilgrimage site had left were abandoned in the atmosphere within its walls, from which something of its sacredness could still be sensed.

Peace is to be found in such moments of recognition, as I experienced then, and have experienced many times since.

After a lengthy previous day of walking around Rome, my desire to lay around and do nothing overcame me and I acquiesced to my body's demands. But there was something more to this fatigue—my mind wanted to rest from all decisions and all traffic of any kind. So I made the choice to do very little and I received immediate benefit.

Prayer, at its core, is a waste of time, as it is a literal wasting of one's time when compared to the models of efficiency and productivity that our world so often relies upon. To make the intentional choice to stop striving to be productive and to unplug from all the busy activity around us, while not just descending into apathy, laziness, or distraction, is to open the door wide to our inner spiritual nature. We often begin to listen in such moments because we have simply turned off the switch that otherwise produces so much noise.

☙

Every year I take a solitude retreat where I spend a few nights in seclusion, with no electronics, nowhere to go and nothing to do. This simple act is typically more than enough to produce long sought-after insights into the deepest recesses of myself. My psyche and its motives are bared to me as I shut out the varied sights and sounds—the endless distractions—that comprise most of my daily life.

Being a modern pilgrim means learning to shut off the noises and distractions of modern society, especially its electronic temptations, in order to locate the richness of oneself and of that which lies beyond us. Wasting time and doing nothing are actually spiritual practices of the highest sort, once we learn to discern their value and not to mistake them as useless or meaningless.

Within this basilica dedicated to Saint Paul, aloof from the rest of the city and offering a solace that most churches its size in Rome simply cannot match, I was returned to a peace easily encountered by letting myself sit at a remove from everything else I had once thought important or necessary. I let the quiet speak to me and I let myself finally listen.

The Tensions of Purgatory

He reflects upon the Museum of Souls in Purgatory in the Sacred Heart of Jesus in Prati—He discusses the Catholic concept of purgatory and a tendency for a both/and logic in the Catholic faith—He expresses his own tensions between the faith of his childhood and the lack of his faith now—He also embraces the both/and principle, letting his tensions co-exist—He also ponders the Catholic question of religious pluralism

THERE ARE OTHER PLACES in Rome where one might recognize seemingly endless tensions.

Rome also contains, for example, the Sacred Heart of Jesus in Prati, or Church of the Sacred Heart of the Suffrage. It is often referred to as the "little Milan Cathedral" for its neo-Gothic style, like the Duomo in Milan—an almost unheard-of architectural style within Rome that is more common in northern Europe. This church is run by the Missionaries of the Sacred Heart, was built in 1917 and consecrated in 1921, and so is a relatively new church among Rome's ancient buildings.

࿓

Inside, and to the right of the altar, in a side hallway, we find a Museum of Souls in Purgatory, as they have framed the somewhat unusual display. This exotic collection began after a fire took place in the old chapel of the Missionaries of the Sacred Heart when the soul of a deceased person was said to have appeared to an attendant there and the effigy of the soul was impressed on a wall or pillar.

To the critical eye, it appears that it was an image left after the fire that merely resembled the head of a man. Victor Jouet, a French priest in the

Missionaries of the Sacred Heart, however, took this image to be evidence of souls in purgatory. Jouet subsequently began to collect relics, prayer books, and many other objects on which images of the departed were said to be imprinted.

Such appeals to these apparently paranormal experiences grant a certain legitimacy to the faith within our modern landscape. As with devotion to the Sacred Heart, there is a call to emotionally ground one's faith in the miraculous, something to which such collections appeal.

☙

Noteworthy in this assortment of the evidences of purgatory are the fingerprints of a soul upon a prayer book and upon a night cap, a photocopied image of an apron with a handprint upon it of a soul stuck in purgatory, and several other finger- or handprints made upon specific objects.

It is not hard to imagine how such images appeal to the Catholic faithful, stirring those living souls who are touched by the mysteries of the afterlife and are looking for certainty amid the uncertainties of human life. It is also another nod toward the popular pieties of the faithful who look for a miraculous occurrence as a sign of faith rather than make the difficult interior journey toward a personal and profound transformation.

Though this may sound like harsh judgment, spiritual writers from Paul to Saint John of the Cross have cautioned Christians not to base their faith on miracles or on some esoteric knowledge, but only on the brokenness and vulnerability that become more evident as one follows the mystery of faith deeper into the experience of Christ's death.

☙

Purgatory enters the Catholic theological lexicon as an attempt to understand how an impure human being could stand in the presence of an entirely pure divinity. Purgatory in fact embodies the act of purifying oneself on their journey to God—a singularly fitting image of the pilgrim extended into speculations on the afterlife. The concept originated in the scriptural, deuterocanonical book of Tobit, where prayers for the dead are mentioned. It subsequently evolved over time from the popular beliefs of ordinary

The Tensions of Purgatory

Catholics into a doctrine concerning how one might stand before God at the end of one's life.

For Saint Bonaventure, purgation was the first stage in approaching God and was followed by illumination and union. One is said to be purified by divine love through a "face-to-face" encounter with God, though it can also be viewed as a "state of existence" rather than as a geographical place.

The Catholic Church today stresses that separation from God, even in the afterlife, is brought about only when humans themselves have chosen it and death merely confirms this decision. Traditionally, suicide was seen as an intentional distancing from God and so a placing of oneself outside of the Catholic community, though this position has since rightly been altered to account for a number of complex factors that might lead a person to take their own life.[1]

❦

Purgatory of course is not to be confused with the idea of limbo, which was traditionally the place where unbaptized babies and virtuous pagans went after their deaths. Limbo was frequently perceived as the first level of hell, where the Roman poet Virgil resided in Dante's *Inferno*. In 2007, however, Pope Benedict XVI essentially repealed the idea of limbo, saying that it presented an unusually restrictive view of salvation.

If the heaven/hell dualism seems to reflect the good/evil ones that humanity utilizes—and oversimplifies—then purgatory is a concept that problematizes this dualism, much like the incarnation problematizes the divine/human boundary and the Trinity problematizes any representations humanity might give of divine being altogether.

❦

Purgatory, in this sense, represents not so much a toleration of ambiguity within Catholic teaching as it does the both/and nature of its philosophy. Catholicism has survived for centuries by adhering to an inclusiveness that the institutional Church itself has struggled to accept at times. The logic of the both/and, however, permeates everything the Church stands for, and has been consistently applied to matters of faith throughout its history.

---

1. O'Collins and Farrugia, *Catholicism*, 217–18, 238–41, 244.

If Protestantism is known for its rigorous application of an either/or mentality—*either* heaven *or* hell, *either* faith *or* works—then Catholicism lives, and thrives, through its embrace of what appears at first as foreign, only to make it into something familiar.

Purgatory, like the doctrine of transubstantiation where bread and wine are said to actually *become* the body of Christ, embodies the principle of the both/and by locating a ground between tacit acceptance and wholesale condemnation, between openness and closedness, between heaven and hell, not merely as a compromised position, but as a true embrace of both positions.

❧

I recall this embodied tension frequently when I walk between the churches of Rome. To be able to hold two contradictory positions in one's mind, without sacrificing the truths offered by each, is a mark of personal maturity, and it is something that individuals, as much as organized religions, should be quicker in embracing as constitutive of their identities.

I personally feel caught in such tensions as that between the faith of my childhood and youth and the lack of religious faith that characterizes my life now, for example. To recognize how this tension is not to be taken as problematic, but as the basis for what "faith" actually is, alters one's understanding of faith altogether, offering new possibilities for the discovery of what truly lies within oneself.

There is a rich complexity to each of our inner worlds and beliefs, and learning to respect those narratives as they co-exist in tension with one another is a crucial step in the maturing of one's life, no matter if it is described as one filled with faith or one removed from traditional forms of religious faith.

❧

When Pope Francis was pressured to canonize Popes John XXIII and John Paul II, icons to liberals and conservatives within the church, respectively, he chose to canonize them *both*, and on the same day. This move was made not just to placate both sides, nor to silence potential criticism; it was a classic maneuver meant to showcase the nature of Catholicism as a whole. Both viewpoints have a place within the larger whole, and these saints' canonizations were indicative of this trend.

It is this same logic that has been deployed on occasion to bring radical saints into the domesticated institution of the Church, subtly transforming the Church from within, even if somewhat blunting the radicality of those saints. I am reminded here especially of the case being made right now for the canonization of Dorothy Day, an American Catholic and founder of the Catholic Worker movement, who once explicitly said that she didn't want to be made into a saint because it would then be easier to "dismiss" her by not hearing the critical nature of her remarks about how one should go about living a Christian life in service to humanity and contrary to the norms of society.

I suspect it might be this same logic that, if opportunely utilized, however, could be the saving grace of the Church itself someday, as an either/or mentality has little room to embrace change.

In a pluralized religious world, Catholicism faces a unique opportunity to embrace other religious traditions and practices, or even a secularized call for none at all, through its application of this both/and inclusiveness. When faced, for example, with the question of religious plurality ("should I be Catholic or Buddhist? Hindu or Muslim?"), the truly Catholic answer might actually be to embrace them all in some sense—and as the Second Vatican Council's document on the world's religions, *Nostra Aetate*, had somewhat begun to do.

Though such a position might seem to signal the death knell of organized religion, it rather appears to me that this may in fact be, or more fully become, Catholicism's lasting gift to the secular world: the ability to sacrifice itself, not through a violent martyrdom that actually undergirds colonialist dreams of imperialist expansion, but through an act of self-renunciation that speaks more to its love of an-other, a love of what is other to it, than a love of itself alone.

As there are no clear guiding principles for the future of religion in a secular age, I would suggest that humanity start here, with an embrace of Catholicism's both/and logic, which can be used not to appropriate or absorb other traditions in the name of one sovereign claim to reality, as in the past, but which can become a model of self-renunciation and openness to a letting go of one's claims, privileges, and even possessions in order to better listen to and navigate an increasingly pluralistic world.

From this vantage point, it is impossible to cling stubbornly to forms of power that are imperial, colonial, racist, sexist, homophobic, and antiquated, to say the least.

Saint Paul's gift to the world at large was his ability to bring competing traditions together. This is not to say that we won't still cling to our particular communal rituals and traditions, or that we won't still idealize a specific religious figure or deity. It is, however, an attempt to reframe the discussion of faith so that we might grasp its true nature within us, and how we might assess and utilize this nature a bit differently than we had before.

The Idol of Perfection

He brings the Villa Medici as an ideal enclosed domestic space into conversation with idealized figures of the saints—He realizes that people aspire to ideals but never actually achieve them—Santa Maria degli Angeli as an example of the Catholic Church rebranding itself—Seeing a lack of divine intervention through the eyes of Galileo—For him, to be open to truth is to be open to one's own errors and vulnerabilities

Villa Medici is the ideal of an enclosed domestic space set apart from everything urban, nonetheless while framing a view of the entire city. It is a monument to elite wealth that is as untouchable as it is decadent. And yet, one can tour its grounds, remark at its splendor, and contextualize it easily within the excessiveness of Rome's own history.

Somewhat ironically, it also calls to mind the legacy of the saints, those divinized humans whose lives are themselves unreal. Or even the desire for something miraculous to occur and perfect those realities we could never complete on our own. We aspire to perfection but will never achieve it. And yet we strive endlessly to be saintly or to be the superhuman (or superhero) who performs truly miraculous deeds.

How does this idealization permeate my desires to be perfect in whatever I do? How is this an ideal that I will never actually achieve? How do I long to leave the groundless ground under the pilgrim's feet, of their self-imposed exile from the everyday, only to realize that I will never actually find the peace I seek, at least not as I envision it?

☙

Religion is often heavily concerned with the fetishizing of an ideal, of a sense of perfection. It can be about trying to control an experience or to possess the unpossessable, even as it loses itself in the mysteriousness and abstraction that always accompanies such longing.

To search for one's voice is as elusive as the idealized body in Greek sculpture or the various statues that litter Rome. Yet to relinquish the desire for such an embodied ideal, as relics or written words seem at times to be, feels like renouncing one's humanity and all its imaginative potential.

All art, as Theodor Adorno once put it, is as fetishistic as any religious longing for enchantment within our material lives, such as we find in religious relics and sacred spaces. We cannot simply dismiss all such constructs as illusions and idols needing to be smashed so that we might finally, at long last, touch the purest presence of the thing itself we are after.[1] There is no ideal we can follow, certainly not one that truly lasts or is eternal.

And yet, persist in our quest for such enchantment we must. Like love, we recognize how fickle such ideals are and yet, at the same time, how much we do need them to provide a guide for us in our lives, a foundation we can take as necessary and permanent, worthy of our trust.

I go on pilgrimage, without even realizing it, to find an idealized version of myself. Somewhere along the journey, however, I learn to let go of even this desire and to make peace with the self that I already am, and will always be. The true ideal, it would seem, is but merely an acceptance of the imperfections that lay within.

At the same time as Christianity started to decline in terms of its retained political power in a modern Western context, a great resurgence of interest arose in ancient Greek and Roman ideals. Some sort of replacement for Christianity had to be sought out in the face of the "death of God" that haunted Western society.

I can appreciate such a resurgence of ancient paths that Western society had let slip off of center stage, and yet I am hesitant to simply dismiss centuries of helpful tradition and practice such as Christianity had frequently produced. Accounting for those problematic parts where one tradition sought to overcome another means learning today to be more

---

1. Adorno, *Aesthetic Theory*.

cautious and less hasty in jettisoning any tradition's claims that have provided a bedrock for so many for so long.

We certainly need new approaches to faith, though we also need to appreciate the beauty of what already went before us. We need at times even to quell the revolutionary and reactionary urges within certain religious quarters in order to champion the slow evolution of reform and the stability that traditions produce over time.

☙

Beauty and tension both reside in the historical clashes between religion and science, witnessed perhaps nowhere more emphatically than in the martyrdom of Giordano Bruno and the imprisonment and censure of Galileo Galilei.

Michelangelo's church near the Baths of Diocletian just a short distance from the Termini train station in the heart of Rome—Santa Maria degli Angeli—contains an impressive spaciousness within itself yet in the midst of ample Roman ruins. It is another example of the Catholic Church rebuilding, and rebranding itself in the process, on top of Roman history.

In this case, the Church made it clear that the Roman "idolaters" were being cast out into the darkness, such as with the inscription still borne there on the walls of the church today: "What was an idol is now a temple of the Virgin / Its creator is the Pious Father himself / Demons begone!"[2]

The triumphalist tone of papal assertions, however, does not wholly detract from the beautiful architectural statement Michelangelo made when converting the space into a sacred, Christian site. Though the interior is somewhat sparse, there is a genuine peacefulness about the place, one that engulfs the faithful and the visitor alike.

☙

The meridian line that runs through the nave functions as a sort of sundial, complete with Zodiac signs in mosaic on the floor. It is creatively designed and singular in its layout, while also reflecting the entrance of a scientific knowledge that sometimes exceeds the Church's own theological agenda.

---

2. Heilbron, *Sun in the Church*, 155.

Charting the course of the sun was, for these early scientist martyrs, a way of learning about truths that the Church often sought to repress. It differs greatly from those immersed in astrology who believe that they are able to read one's fate in the stars and so to be in control of one's own life to some degree, as when life often feels well beyond one's control. Both have appeared as contradictions to the Church's interpretation of divine Providence, and both have been sought—and still are sought—as alternatives to the monopoly on fate that the Church has seemed almost destined at times to dictate.

For the pilgrim, these tensions represent an interesting distraction, but also a clarification for guidance: not trying to gain control over one's fate and yet being open to the presentation of truth no matter where it appears are both fundamental to the journey itself.

Not wanting to see the truth, not wanting even to acknowledge its presence, has been severely detrimental to the Church's sense of itself, as it has often chosen to hide its fears and repress the truth before its eyes rather than acknowledge the extent to which a particular truth might cause it to reframe a good many of its assumptions.

The pilgrim, it should be restated, must move away from any desire to let one's fears guide them and away from any desire to repress whatever truth must face the light of day.

So many of us wish there were a plan or order to our existence, that our fate was marked by divine will or by the stars above, and that if we simply demonstrated enough faith we could glimpse our destiny if only for a glorious moment. The idea that we are in control of our own lives, that we dwell in a boundless freedom, is an overwhelming and impossible notion, one that seems buffeted on every side by the contingent acts that take place around us and have a significant impact on us every day.

The pilgrim is the one who walks directly into such daily contingencies while also witnessing to the resilience to remain focused on one's reason for being here rather than whatever offers to take us away from the hardship of the journey itself.

The Idol of Perfection

Even if the route I take has no particular destination, I treat the journey as if the end were a necessary conclusion to every uncertainty I embody. I walk as if destiny guided my steps and every encounter becomes fused with a sacred aura.

To be clear, I do not believe in destiny of fate or a divine plan that oversees our lives "from above." I do not believe in a deity who might govern our fates like a puppet master in the sky. But I believe in living as if such things existed.

There is purpose to our lives and meaning to be found in the stories we tell ourselves about ourselves. There is meaning in reading our lives from the situation we find ourselves in as if what came to pass had to take place in precisely such a way.

Embracing one's life as if there were no other way it could have come to pass is an acknowledgment of the significance and uniqueness of one's own life, in all of its wonderful complexity. It is an act of choosing one's life as a choosing of one's destiny. This is how we, in some measure, gain control over the uncontrollable while rereading religious impulses as fundamentally very human ones. This is also how we learn to acknowledge our all too human thoughts and actions as essentially religious at the same time.

ב

I find it odd that we are often drawn to purify or cleanse ourselves of habits, routines, diets, and patterns of thought, but not of religious faith, when such a loss may actually be not only an incredibly helpful cleansing of ourselves, but something that takes us to the heart of what religious experience is actually about, therefore allowing us to return to it in some measure as well.

To encounter the divine is to be bereft of all of our normal capacities for understanding, to admit a sense of loss that is yet constitutive of sacred experience and encounter. To embrace a loss of faith might actually become the most authentic way to locate faith once again, even if it ends up looking nothing like what we had thought it should be.

Since I was a child, I wondered why a Christian would be afraid to face the hard, critical truths of reason, for truth is truth no matter its source or application. To be open to truth, in whatever form it takes, is to be open to one's own errors and vulnerabilities, which certainly includes the loss of what we hold dear.

As a pilgrim in this world, I have often learned how important it is to listen to the truths being told from whatever quarter in which they appear, and to let them reshape me without fear or anxiety distracting me from a purposeful engagement with the world around me, and with myself.

I cannot imagine what strength of character it must have taken to adhere to scientific truths when faced with the sheer might of an incredibly hierarchical and powerful religious organization bent on dismissing one's views. I also cannot imagine the humiliation that a religious institution bears when it is forced to recant its own errors and to rethink its understanding of how the world works.

Taking the time to let the shame of one's actions permeate one's existence, to confess one's wrongs publicly, and to place oneself along a better route to complete the journey before them, these are the significant tasks both personal and institutional that we all must face.

༄

The church's meridian line finds its fitting intellectual complement in the statue of Galileo (installed in 2010) that resides just outside the sacristy of Santa Maria degli Angeli. Titled *Galileo Galilei Divine Man*, by Tsung Dao Lee, it reminds us all of the tensions between science and faith.

It is of course deeply ironic that Galileo, a man hounded and haunted by the Catholic Church's refusal to see the truth before their eyes, should now be honored in one of the most historic locations of Roman Catholicism, but such are the ironies of history.

The fact that I find myself, technically a professor of Catholic theology, becoming more content with my own lack of religious belief while learning deeply from the churches of Rome is yet another. I know all too well the desire to want to be a part of a plan much larger than myself and of wanting to believe that one's purpose is given to us by a divine and loving hand. But wanting it to be so and it actually being so are two very different things.

There are, of course, numerous poetic ways in which religious symbols and myths speak profound truths to humankind on the whole, but there are also violent and damaging political theological legacies within religion that need to be isolated and opposed.

I will never know the rejection and fear that must have characterized the lives of Bruno and Galileo, the torment, abuse, and ignorance that was repeatedly thrown at them. I will never have to experience being banned from teaching, having my writings burnt, being placed under arrest, or, as in Bruno's case, being killed for my beliefs.

But I know the social pressure to pretend as if the claims of divine revelation were true in ways that they are not. This force is real and it has shaped too many of my actions already in the short life that I have lived.

The Truth of Martyrdom

He reflects on the martyrdoms near the Pasquino statue in Piazza Navona—He goes on to describe the history of martyrdom in the early church—For him, the martyrs are the ones who ground themselves in their faith through an absurd choice—On the one hand, the martyr is an inspiration for the pilgrim who makes a foolish decision to waste their time and effort from the first moment of their journey—On the other hand, he also finds several differences between the martyr and the pilgrim

THE TRUNCATED STATUE OF Pasquino just off the Piazza Navona is said to always speak the truth, which is why hard truths often appear written next to the statue. Truthful words written here have often been aimed throughout the centuries at the pope and various political leaders needing to hear the truths being spoken to them.

I like to think that the Pasquino statue finds its twin in the giant statue of Giordano Bruno located not far across the street in the middle of the Campo de' Fiori.

Bruno lost his life at the hands of the Church by refusing to retract the scientific truths he discovered and subsequently spoke to the Catholic hierarchy. Though today's Catholic Church has fared somewhat better in its relations to scientific truths—including John Paul II's acceptance of evolutionary theory, for example—it does no better by discriminating against women and denying them a role in its priesthood, among other contemporary social issues the Church faces today.

By speaking out repeatedly on the roles and dignity of women in the Church while saying nothing about men or the perilous temptations of men (as abusers and potential rapists in particular), the Church continues to lose credibility within a world intent on embracing ever expanding forms of equality. It is a strange but real phenomenon that the Church continues to lose influence because of its refusal to adapt to the times, but such is the case at the moment.

⁂

If we must re-envision martyrdom today in light of these martyrs to the truths of scientific inquiry, then we might perhaps start our inquiry near the Pasquino statue, in the Piazza Navona, site of numerous martyrdoms throughout history.

The late evening charm of the Piazza Navona, at the heart of Rome's oldest quarter, is abundant upon encountering it from any number of narrow side streets leading to it. Coming upon its open expanse contains a subtle joy, as if wandering from narrow to narrower streets had suddenly yielded a hidden gem.

⁂

At its center is the "Fountain of the Four Rivers" by Gian Lorenzo Bernini (1651), which, with its slender obelisk on top supported underneath by four angled columns, allegedly inspired the shape of the Eiffel Tower in Paris.

The obelisks, in general, were markers for pilgrims of significant Christian sites in Rome, as well as obvious signs of papal power. Rome has the largest number of obelisks in the world, including eight ancient Egyptian ones, five ancient Roman ones, and many modern ones. Roman emperors liked to bring the Egyptian ones to Rome in order to assert their own divine status and to emphasize how the ever expanding Roman empire surpassed Egypt's prior dominance in history.

Like the Pantheon—a Roman temple to all the gods now converted into a church—the obelisks have an ambiguous relationship to Christianity. It is never clear to the astute observer if Christianity is appropriating the alleged divinity of the pharaoh/emperor for itself or whether some merger unseen has taken place between varied forms of the sacred.

The piazza, for all of its glory, however, conceals a darker past in the immediacy of its present exuberance. Underneath the light-colored façades of the conjoined buildings that run along its outer edges, the lingering presence of a Roman stadium and of many early Christian martyrdoms penetrates its historical consciousness. Indeed, the large open space of the piazza is a reminder of the ancient stadium's course track structure.

☙

Pope Fabian (d. 250) was one of the first popes to be martyred during the Roman persecutions of Christians, and his death signaled the difficulties of being a Christian in the first few centuries of the Church's history. Christians at this time were often arrested and condemned to death in a variety of ways.

For their part, Christians were frequently divided on whether to conceal their faith, and so to hide from prying authorities, or whether to prominently display their faith as an act of witness and courage, despite the eminent death that was likely to result from such exposure. The cost of handling matters wrongly was significant. Pope Marcellinus, for example, renounced the Christian faith and sacrificed to pagan gods, dying in disgrace in 304.[1]

Martyrdom in the early church was often an immediate cause for one's sainthood, and the blood of the martyrs is frequently referred to as "seeds of the Church," as the ancient church father Tertullian had put it.

The Roman Church, for its part, was so eager to lift up courageous stories of martyrdom that it even poached stories of martyrs from other parts of the world and attempted to relocate them to Rome.[2]

☙

Certain early martyrdom stories remain controversial, however, to such a degree that theologians debated at the time, and have quite a few times since then, as to whether a Christian welcoming martyrdom was actually completing some form of suicide.

This issue is still debated by certain evangelical missionaries today, especially as they have to watch those from among their ranks try to spread the gospel to remote corners of the world the way early Catholic missionaries once did but have now basically ceased to do. In some cases, such as

---

1. Duffy, *Saints and Sinners*, 20.
2. Taylor, Rinne, and Kostof, *Rome*, 139.

when they attempt to reach out to remote indigenous tribes who defend themselves against intruders, they put their lives at risk in ill-advised ways.

Donatism, an early Church group labeled as heretical for their positions regarding this very issue, formed itself as a theological movement aimed against those who renounced their faith in order to avoid martyrdom. Donatists essentially believed that you forfeited your salvation if you recanted your beliefs in the face of an eminent death. Such "traitors" had compromised the validity of the sacraments, which had to be maintained in their purity at all costs.

Interestingly, however, the Donatist position, despite its striving to represent an orthodox view, was eventually denied by the Church, which chose not to link a priest's holiness to the validity of the sacraments. God, it seems, is bigger than any human inclination.

&

So why was Christianity persecuted by the Roman Empire specifically, creating so many martyrs, such as were killed throughout Rome and in the Piazza Navona in particular?

In the early Church, Christian openness to unconventional relationships (for example, women's roles, seeing servants as equal to their masters, a favoring of adoption over naturally conceived children, opposition to abortion, and so forth) worked steadily to subvert Roman familial-patriarchal ("household") religious structures. Rather than uphold the economic and cultural status quo, the poor were uplifted as "treasures of the Church," as Saint Lawrence had once phrased things, to be cared for by those within the Church.

Monotheism itself too was typically an *exclusive* rival claim to Roman imperial rule and its divinity, the emperor. Only one deity could reign supreme. Hence, the early Christian theologian Irenaeus stressed the unity of God *and* God's people, rejected heretical and Roman pagan views, defined orthodoxy as unity itself, stressed Jesus' role in bringing God to humanity through Mary's submission to God's will, and demonstrated the goodness of humanity as the image of God. These early efforts toward ecclesial unity were given a unique twist when Constantine utilized them to unite the Roman Empire through Christian claims.[3]

---

3. O'Collins and Farrugia, *Catholicism*, 17–18, 21.

The ideal of martyrdom frequently appears within various religious traditions as the noblest of passionate ideals. An individual willing to give up their life for a truth they cannot renounce without compromising the way they live their life is a deeply powerful sentiment, however corrupt its intentions may be. Many uncompromising religious persons resonate with the martyrs for just this reason. Hence, the life of the true believer, one willing to become a martyr, is forfeit if they are not able to adhere to the beliefs that make their life worth living.

Martyrs are an inspiration unlike any other for just this reason. Like the deaths of those soldiers who prop up fidelity to a particular nation-state, the religious martyr automatically becomes a saint to the cause, a steadfast reason why the truth of religion, in numerous global contexts, endures for many today.

୬

Martyrs are, however, more than just the means by which truth is conveyed, more than a defense of that truth: they embody the structure of how a groundless truth develops and cultivates its own foundations. They are, in this sense, the forerunners of so many religious persons who seek endlessly to justify their faith through recourse to ultimately ungroundable positions, often captured in phrases such as the tautological "I believe because I believe because I believe."

The martyr seemingly justifies the faith they profess through their militant fidelity to it, giving it a grounding that it would otherwise have struggled to obtain for itself. The reality that some religions, as with some political causes, have an abundance of foolish martyrs whose deaths inspired others to emulate their vain and useless actions, as the cause itself was entirely bankrupt, should alert us to the possibility of corrupt conditions that martyrdom attempts to legitimate.

The martyr's truth, faith's truth really, is that an individual can ground the faith, *their* faith, through death, by simply willing it to be so. Faith becomes manifest, becomes *real*, through a powerful act of willing it to be real, much as love becomes real through the act of intensely loving someone.

୬

There is nothing inherently within a religious tradition that can justify or legitimate the religion itself. It is only through an act of will, or belief, that faith can sustain itself over time. The faith of the martyr, as a self-referential act, is the basis *of* faith, not simply a legitimation *for* faith. There is truly no justification one can give for sacrificing their life for their beliefs. The martyr's death will always defy reason because it discloses a passionate attachment beyond reason's hold.

But this is precisely the point of the act of the martyr itself: it is only through such an absurd, irrational choice that one can ground themselves in their faith (as one might in their love for another person). The martyr thereby embodies the logic that sustains religious belief the world over. They provide the most fitting image of what grounding something that is ultimately groundless looks like, by making an unreasonable sacrifice to legitimate belief itself.

Except for the occasional misguided missionary who believes they can convert the "natives" to faith, or their warped vision of a "true faith," the modern period has seen a steady retreat from the logic of martyrdom as the basis of one's faith. For this reason, faith itself suffers and declines, because there is no other way to describe or encapsulate the irrational rationale for faith than with the sacrifice offered by the martyr.

Yet the logic of the martyr becomes harder and harder to justify in an age of religious plurality where dying for one's faith seems more ludicrous than merely antiquated. Why an individual should die for a particular belief rather than another equally implausible belief relativizes the nature of religious truth. It is not a coincidence, moreover, that romanticized notions of love have increased at the same time, as they offer a parallel narrative of the willingness to sacrifice oneself for a particular, and completely unjustifiable, relationship.[4]

Human beings will always have a need to legitimate their beliefs through self-referential acts of willing, but the age of martyrdom seems to be fast approaching its end, despite whatever a handful of radicalized fanatics in multiple religious traditions still proclaim.

---

4. See the argument made in May, *Love*.

Sacred Pilgrim, Secular Pilgrim

The decline of interest in martyrdom is no doubt a sign of the modern age in which we live, when the irrational, passionate attachments that we cannot do without—such as with religious belief, but also with our loves and commitments, from the patriotic to the romantic—have come under a critical eye that can be incredibly dismissive of such bonds.

To be fair, many of our most passionate commitments do need to be re-examined and even removed from our lives, especially when they promote or condone abusive or violent actions.

To try to remove them permanently from our lives, however, would like be trying to breathe without oxygen—a certain death of all that makes us human.

For every religiously inspired act of evil, there is another committed believer who seeks to help others purely out of an abundant love for humanity. For every unjustifiable atrocity that takes place due to misguided religious beliefs and commitments, there is the unjustifiable act of charity that promotes the wealth of those irrational choices that yet ground us in our own lives.

&

The martyr, in this sense, is an inspiration for the pilgrim, who makes the irrational decision to push their body through space in order to somehow, unknown to themselves, ground their existence within their own embodied state of being. The choice to be a pilgrim and to walk to destinations both known and unknown in the hopes of healing, forgiveness, encounter, relationship, and love, seems so illogical as to be suspect from the start. The pilgrim makes a foolish decision to waste their time and effort from the moment they begin their journey.

Unlike the martyrs who die for causes that only serve to reinforce an already fragile sense of self by trying to overcome it through their level of commitment, the pilgrim, akin to other types of martyrs, loosens their identity and admits their ungroundedness—their true homelessness—in order to move that much closer to the reality of their own existence. There is, in such acts, a willingness to expose their vulnerability with and through their bodies, bearing their passionate attachments with everything they have, though not to legitimate their social, political, and religious identities, but to open themselves up to a mystery that far exceeds any label one might put upon them, a label that they care nothing for anyway.

The Truth of Martyrdom

Inspiration comes to us in so many different ways, often through impulses and insights that we are unable to see the source of. I listen to the stories of those willing to give their lives for their faith and I am inspired when I see how what grounded them in their beliefs was the same willingness to be stripped of everything they had held dear so that they might locate something so much more precious beyond whatever they possessed. If such actions are not the most direct embodiment of love, then we will never learn much of anything about what love can be.

Grounding the Ungroundable

He views and reflects upon the murals of martyrdom at Santo Stefano Rotondo and the church of S. Agnese in Agone—For him, faith is a relationship that attempts to ground the ungroundable—He also admits that faith is an interpersonal thing in which family and community are its center—Viewing the murals of the martyrs, he feels that faith is presented through art as clearly as if seen through relics

THIS REALITY OF MARTYRDOM, both historically and today, makes it difficult to view the murals of martyrdom at Santo Stefano Rotondo in Rome. For example, it is difficult to muster any sort of passionate commitment on par with the seventeenth-century Jesuit missionaries who first viewed them while contemplating the potentially violent fates that lay ahead of them in pursuit of global missionary work. We lack their conviction because we lack their context.

We are far more fixated today on the sacrifices called for in romantic love, as we have loosened the bonds of religious longing and placed a burden on romance so great that it may not always be able to bear the strain of our expectations.[1]

Christendom, mainly, no longer maintains its overt imperial claims to sovereign global and colonialist rule. The desire to impose a Western European hegemonic viewpoint upon the peoples of the world in the name of Christ looms less largely than it once did, and so the violence of conversion, at times accompanying forced conversions and prayers for the conversion of "wayward peoples" like the Jews, need not be justified by the violent deaths of those martyrs who appeared to be the only fitting counterpart to the converted.

---

1. See the argument presented on romantic love in May, *Love*.

Grounding the Ungroundable

Both violences have decreased, and in some cases disappeared altogether, because they are derivative of the same source. The same violence runs directly through them both.

※

Faith is a relationship and as such it attempts to, and at times does, ground the ungroundable: the intimacy between persons that is one of the most fragile and illusory, yet absolutely necessary and foundational elements in human life. Religion is for this reason an essential part of humanity's existence on this planet and it cannot, for the very reason that it speaks the same language as lovers do, be easily eradicated.

Religion is therefore often deeply misunderstood when analyzed under the modern, critical microscope, for its mythological narratives and supernatural claims are easily and hastily rejected as contrary to scientific and historical truths, while the language that religion actually speaks is more akin to poetry. We would never dare to ask questions of historical, factual veracity to a poem in order to judge its legitimacy as a poem, and yet we dismiss religious speech for not addressing a particular genre of discourse—historical, factual truth—that it was never intended to buttress.

※

This confusion, seen for what it is, is a category mistake and it is what enables me to be a theologian and to take religion more seriously than ever, even as I profess my lack of belief at the same time. This is not a contradiction to me, though I am sure it will appear so to many.

Taking this position is an inherently isolated one at the same time, of course, because it rejects the traditional means of justifying one's identity and community to and for others. There are no absolute grounds for claiming allegiance to one community over another, *any* other, while also recognizing that theological and metaphysical arguments are historically what have been used to argue for just such a foundation.

The poetry that religion speaks at its symbolic core is like the poetry of a people or a land, speaking a single language whose beauty is only unveiled slowly through its sacred use.

Sacred Pilgrim, Secular Pilgrim

To be in my position is to recognize the beauty of this sacred language of passionate commitment while also standing at a certain remove from its practice. My community is ultimately to be found elsewhere, among random associations of friendship, but borrowing always from the religious traditions of my own upbringing.

※

I don't write as much or as often, nor do I have the space for as much reflection in general, when I am traveling with other people, as I am right now with my parents in Rome. This could be an obvious source of frustration since I am often lured away from the pilgrim's focus by so many things that are sure to arise when others are needing attention.

At the same time, however, I recognize fully how faith at its core is about relationships and about how those whom we love are most often the ones who cause us to feel accepted, loved, as if we truly belonged. They lift up our uniqueness and honor the individual spirits that we are, but which we sometimes need reminding of.

Faith is an interpersonal thing, something that cannot be sustained without those who foster and reflect the love we feel in our lives. Being a pilgrim in the midst of others is therefore not a dissolution of its many dimensions, but another one to add to the unending list of its traits.

As with everyone, we do not know how long we will be able to experience the joys and despairs of life with those we love. To get a chance to travel as a pilgrim with one's loved ones is a uniqueness that cannot be passed over, even if the challenges it presents have to be more directly balanced by the gifts that we are also given.

Family and community are central to religious faith, even if pilgrimage is often a solitary exercise, just as retreats, spiritual direction, and confession are often personal and private. Pilgrimage is, in this sense, always engaged in a dialectic between personal meditation and communal solidarity. We drift far from home to see our "being at home" differently, to return to our communities and daily lives restored and replenished, ready to see things differently and to take up life anew.

※

The church of S. Agnese in Agone, in the middle of Piazza Navona, is a shrine to the martyrs whose lives deeply populate the Roman-Christian lore of the earliest church communities and the love they bore for one another. Under an impressively stunning dome, the ornate church has become something of a museum while trying yet to direct visitors toward its adoration of Agnes's short life and graphic martyrdom.

The choice of dramatic stone reliefs to tell the various stories of the martyrs within each side chapel is likewise striking, as if the figures were trying to leap out from the walls and tell their stories directly to the viewer. The evangelization of the masses that was so important to St. Philip Neri could be said to be displayed here to perfection.

Neri, whose baroque Chiesa Nuova ("New Church") lies just around the corner from this church, is the saint who popularized religious devotion during the sixteenth century, leading pilgrims to the seven pilgrim churches throughout the city.

The New Church is itself an immense Baroque building with an impressive array of art, marble and gold. It is easy to see how this church was at one time the gem in Rome's new font of evangelization to the world, building off of the legacy of martyrs from the Piazza Navona and leading into an age of significant missionary expansion. From its artwork, originally including a Caravaggio painting above one of its side altars, to its focus on liturgy and devotion, this church captures the imagination of faith and brings it to its liturgical center point.

The lingering presence of martyrdom on the Piazza Navona, however, is rendered palpable by the graphic murals of various martyrs that circumnavigate the inner walls of Santo Stefano Rotondo, a mausoleum-like structure a short distance from the Colosseum that is meant to endear the church's many martyrs to the living faithful. Wandering through the sanctuary feels like you are actually traipsing about an interior courtyard in some ways. The round shape of the church was apparently modeled after imperial mausoleums that were generally built to honor a specific hero, but the structure of this church is highly unusual and has led to much speculation as to its origins, which may have had something to do with the cult of Mithras.

In many of its cathedrals, such as is explicitly championed at Santa Croce, or "Holy Cross," which I will discuss later, Catholicism often attempts to provide a "catechesis of the relics," utilizing material objects to teach the faith. This technique for presenting the faith is a reminder of the sacramental imagination in the Catholic world, wherein the materiality of rituals and traditions, of saints and martyrs, reaches out to the spiritual dimension so that the spiritual can be infused with the material.

The murals of the martyrs are another reminder, along with the works of Fra Angelica, Caravaggio, and so many other artists throughout Rome, of how the faith is presented through art as clearly as it is through relics. Together, relics, icons, the bodies of the saints, paintings, sculpture, and even stained glass are profound reminders of how Catholicism presents to the world a profoundly embodied faith.

No matter how we might try to escape the material conditions of our faith, and of our very lives, we are constantly reminded that such gestures toward greater abstraction are always countered by embodied realities all around us.

The pilgrim embraces the fusion of material and spiritual because there is no other way to go deeper into understanding one's own self and the selves of those around them. To claim that only the spiritual matters—as Protestantism has often been historically tempted to do—is to miss the larger reality that can only be ignored at our peril.

༄

The murals of Stefano Rotondo themselves were commissioned in 1583 by Pope Gregory XIII, according to new policies within the Church to make iconography more realistic. In this way individual saints might be recognizable and their deeds inspiring to those contemplating their own willingness—or unwillingness—to stand up for their faith when encountering new cultures around the world heretofore unknown to Western civilization.

The paintings were also a direct counter-Reformation initiative, since the parallel between Catholic martyrs and Protestantism's critiques and persecutions of Catholics would have been obvious to Catholics at the time.[2] The Council of Trent, which the Catholic Church had called to order so that they might deal with Reformation tendencies and movements, had

---

2. Hughes, *Rome*, 177.

recommended using visual teaching methods to spread the faith, and this church in particular responded accordingly.

The paintings also gave Jesuit missionaries, among others, a potential taste of what they might encounter globally in spreading the Christian faith. Jesuit missionary efforts had been expanding tremendously since the order's beginnings in the sixteenth century, famously including Francis Xavier's travels to India in the footsteps of the apostle Thomas, as well as to China, José de Anchieta and Peter Claver's trips to South America, Alessandro Valignano's mission work in Japan, and Matteo Ricci's work in China. Later Jesuit missionaries would also include Pierre-Jean de Smet's forays in North America and a host of others who were martyred while trying to spread the gospel to various native American tribes.

The Council of Trent was not only an attempt to stem the tide of the Reformation; it also sought to reform the Catholic Church from within, including its many corruptions at the hands of various Renaissance popes. Called by Pope Paul III in 1545, it sought to critically examine the moral ills that infested the Vatican, including a corrupt college of cardinals. Paul III's accomplice in this mission was Cardinal Caraffa, the eventual Pope Paul IV, who is buried at S. Maria sopra Minerva in Rome. The latter was a ruthless character who, for instance, instituted numerous Inquisitions in order to violently suppress heresy within the Church.[3]

Nonetheless, when Trent resumed after Paul IV's suspension of it, the council was able to effective promote a counter-Reformation agenda, in which the Jesuits had a major role to play. The college of cardinals was further diluted and rendered increasingly powerless by the appointment of many more cardinals, especially poor ones who would not be corrupted as easily.[4] After the Council of Trent, however, the papacy became a major authoritarian, absolutist, and centralized office.[5]

Perhaps because the period in which the murals came to life was so stark and chaotic, the images that line the walls of Santo Stefano Rotondo

---

3. Duffy, *Saints and Sinners*, 210.

4. Duffy, *Saints and Sinners*, 222. We might think here too of the Jesuit Pope Francis's reforming of the Curia today, and his appointment of many cardinals from poor global locations, a clear echo of these tactics.

5. Duffy, *Saints and Sinners*, 223.

are as bold as they are gruesome and disturbing. In one art commentator's words, "These 16th-century murals show Roman martyrs being flayed, boiled, vivisected, roasted, crucified, and buried alive. The name of the emperor who ordered each type of torture appears above each mural." Included are Saint Thecla, torn by bulls; Saint Ignatius, thrown to the lions; Saints Gervase and Protase nailed to trees; and Saint Eustachius roasted alive in a bronze bull.[6]

The British novelist Charles Dickens visited the church at one point and later wrote about his experience:

> To single out details from the great dream of Roman Churches, would be the wildest occupation in the world. But St. Stefano Rotondo, a damp, mildewed vault of an old church in the outskirts of Rome, will always struggle uppermost in my mind, by reason of the hideous paintings with which its walls are covered. These represent the martyrdoms of saints and early Christians; and such a panorama of horror and butchery no man could imagine in his sleep, though he were to eat a whole pig raw, for supper. Grey-bearded men being boiled, fried, grilled, crimped, singed, eaten by wild beasts, worried by dogs, buried alive, torn asunder by horses, chopped up small with hatchets: women having their breasts torn with iron pinchers, their tongues cut out, their ears screwed off, their jaws broken. . . . So insisted on, and laboured at, besides, that every sufferer gives you the same occasion for wonder as poor old Duncan awoke, in Lady Macbeth, when she marvelled at his having so much blood in him.[7]

As you walk around the circular interior of the church, the images begin to pour off the walls, provoking each viewer with the seriousness of faith as embodied in the various persons who would rather have undergone torture and death than recant their beliefs.

Symbolically and literally, the portraits of the martyrs begin with Mary, the mother of Christ, and the seven swords said to pierce her heart—a reference to her encounter in the Gospel of Luke with a prophet named Simeon who foresaw that her heart would be pierced with a sword due to the suffering she would experience during her son's life and death. The phrase "Our Lady of Sorrows" tries, in its own way, to capture the imagined

---

6. Hughes, *Rome*, 177.
7. Dickens, *Pictures from Italy*, 136.

pain of her heart being pierced by each new suffering she witnessed her son bearing.[8]

Mary's suffering lays the psychological foundation for Jesus' own martyrdom, an act that every subsequent martyrdom mirrors. Saint Stephan, to note, is considered the first martyr of the church, and his stoning, which took place immediately after a passionate speech given in defense of Jesus' life and teachings, was witnessed by Saul who later became Paul sometime around the year 34.[9] Stephen's relics were said to be moved to this very location, but there is no evidence that this ever actually happened.

The martyrs Primus and Felicianus were, however, reburied here sometime around 460 after being moved from their resting place in the catacombs on the edge of the city. A chapel was subsequently dedicated to them, demonstrating once again how central the concept of the martyr was to the early church.

Most of the early apostles were martyred for following Jesus, including James, Stephen, Peter, Paul, Philip, Andrew, Jude, and Thomas, among others. The early church, likewise, was full of significant martyrs, such as Polycarp, Justin Martyr, Perpetua and Felicity, Sebastian, and Ignatius of Antioch. Even the city of Rome itself has a series of martyrs who illuminate the unique history of Christianity in Rome: Lucy, Lawrence, Cecilia, and Agnes make up just some of this famous list.

Since many have subsequently altered their take on martyrdom in the modern period, one is left to wonder at times if figures such as Giordano Bruno, who, through his refusal to recant his "heretical" scientific views before the Roman Inquisition, was burned at the stake in 1600 on the Campo de' Fiori, might qualify today as a Roman martyr.

---

8. The traditional seven sorrows she experienced include: (1) the stunning nature of Simeon's prophecy itself, (2) the family's fleeing into Egypt, (3) the loss of Jesus for three days when he was a child, (4) her encounter with Jesus on the way to Calvary and his death, (5) the crucifixion itself, (6) her taking his body down from the cross, and, finally, (7) the burial of her son before his resurrection.

9. Acts 6–7.

The Idol of Purity

He focuses on Saints Agnese and Cecilia who are idealized in their martyrdoms for upholding faith—The potential misleading idealizations of purity and holiness in young, female, virgin martyrs—He adds that martyrdom was the means to give a voice to the voiceless against their oppressors

WHAT WE CHOOSE TO bury within history, to repress and ignore, often returns to us in profound, if at times ambiguous, ways. This was what I felt, not simply thought, as I descended another stairway into another catacomb underneath a church dedicated to a young female martyr.

I was held in an almost hypnotic state by the fact of the catacomb, by its unrelenting push backward in history, the knowledge that it had once touched something like the origins of a faith billions still shared.

I didn't choose for the catacombs to jump-start this spiral into memory; I don't believe anyone ever does. A few meager bills pressed into someone's hand had admitted us to the English tour, and we descended backward, downward, into hollow spaces carved long ago into rock. It was an amazement, both my students and I were told, that they could technically engineer such things at that point in history, in secret, through faith, with not much more than their faith to guide them.

But what was this to us? What could such a thing be to us anymore? What was shared between such people? What stories had leaked through the shallow earth and seeped into the rock, had torn chunks of it away and deposited themselves in little pools amidst the bones and the living workers who placed them there?

The Idol of Purity

Founded in 342, but later rebuilt, Sant'Agnese fuori le mura is named for Saint Agnes, who was martyred at the young age of thirteen in 304 on the Piazza Navona, and whose name graces the church there, as I already mentioned.

Agnes, historians tell us, was actually martyred on the site of a brothel that had once been near the stadium, as prostitutes generally hung around such stadiums, under the arches (*fornices*, etymologically linked to "fornication") that surrounded them. As another etymology attests, the prostitutes also used to eat a quick dish of pasta now called "pasta alla puttanesca" (from *puttane*, or prostitute).[1]

Agnes is the patron saint of young girls and all female rape survivors, mainly because her story suggests that she was led to a brothel in order to have her virginity taken from her shortly before her death, though her captors, as the legend goes, were unable to accomplish this heinous act.

It is important to recall at this point that Agnes means "pure," a true sign of the symbolic and moral nature of her tale. She is in fact the patron saint of chastity and, due to her purity, is frequently associated with white lambs.[2]

When exposed naked in the brothel, her hair was said to have quickly and miraculously grown quite long in order to cover over her entire body, thus preserving her purity in the face of potential defilement. For this, she is also, and somewhat oddly, the patron saint of gardeners.

The original building for Sant'Agnese outside the walls may have been a funerary complex rather than a basilica, especially considering that the grounds also contain the fourth-century Mausoleum of Santa Costanza, otherwise known as Constantina, the daughter of the Roman Emperor Constantine.

---

1. Hughes, *Rome*, 348.

2. She is often depicted in iconography with a lamb, the name of which in Latin, "agnus," sounds like "Agnes."

The catacombs directly underneath Sant'Agnese were built because early Christians wanted to be buried somewhere where they would be close to her in their own deaths. This practice parallels the desire to place a saint's body underneath the main altar of a church, as I have already noted, with catacombs branching out underneath. The building of Sant'Agnese itself was therefore constructed on the level of the catacombs, so you go downward from street level to enter the church.

The church contains the relics of both St. Agnes and St. Emerentiana, the daughter of Agnes's nanny and wet-nurse, who was stoned to death while visiting Agnes's grave. Both young women are idealized in their martyrdoms for upholding their faith, and the seventh-century apse mosaic reflects this historical detail by portraying Agnes being handed the crown of martyrdom, signifying a major accomplishment through her death and the maintenance of her purity despite the many attacks that were made against her.

The prominence of the female virgin martyrs is palpable when one simply steps into the church's sanctuary, as many of their portraits are located near the upper windows, placed just above a series of papal images. The contrast is somewhat stark: young female virgin martyrs to be admired for their purity and loyalty to Christ and the Church juxtaposed with aging male popes who were often as devious and ruthless as they were models of indecency. Even in this church dedicated to a female saint, the male hierarchy asserts itself.

The central figures in the ceiling include Saints Agnes and Cecilia, each wearing a halo as their crown, but also Costanza, who features no halo, but does wear a royal crown.

To my mind, however, questions remained: what does it mean that Agnes is lifted up as a saintly model of purity and holiness, dying a virgin and martyr? How is the image of purity placed upon women within the Church's history and how is this being challenged today?

The Idol of Purity

The tension between purity and impurity regarding women is especially intriguing when seen in contrast with the male hierarchy of the Catholic Church. How is this tension to be absorbed in light of other tensions between rich and poor (or rich churches and poor churches), hierarchy (monarchy) and egalitarianism (democracy), or Christology and pneumatology? Are these virginal saints women who should be emulated, or do they set unrealistic expectations of purity for women today?

☙

Supposedly built over the house (*domus ecclesia*) of Santa Cecilia, who was martyred in 177, it now appears that there was not a house church on the site of another church dedicated to a young female martyr, Santa Cecilia in Trastevere. Rather a Roman pagan shrine that was popular under the reign of Marcus Aurelius lays beneath it. Perhaps, as well, it might have been a grain storage facility at one point in time. But her relics were moved here from the San Callisto catacombs in the ninth century and the church has dominated the space ever since. Cecilia has been celebrated liturgically with a feast day since the fourth century and her story is the stuff of legend.

In its most basic form, we are told that she was forced to marry a Roman nobleman, Valerian, whom she did not want to marry. During their wedding, she stayed off to the side singing to herself—becoming the patron saint of music as a consequence. She allegedly told her husband that if he tried to consecrate their marriage by sleeping with her, an angel would harm him. His disbelief resulted in her saying to him that if he traveled the Via Appia to a certain point outside the city and was later baptized as a Christian, he would see the angel for himself, which he later did after completing these tasks.

As the hagiography goes, they remained chaste throughout their marriage, a point that must have gone some ways toward earning Valerian his eventual sainthood as well. However, sometime later, the pair was rounded up by Roman soldiers and executed simply for being Christian, though Cecilia was first left in a bathhouse to suffocate. Failing to fully suffocate her, though, she was to be beheaded with three axe blows, which also failed to do the job, leaving her to languish for three days before finally dying.

She is often remembered alongside Agnes as one of the greatest Roman virgin martyrs, their lives becoming even more intertwined after their deaths. For example, not only is there an ornate, Gothic style crypt underneath the main altar with mosaics linking Cecilia with Agnes, but the Benedictine nuns who live here today create the pallium of sheep's wool that is worn by the pope and other bishops of high rank. It is a stole that is made at Santa Cecilia and blessed at the church of Sant'Agnese before going on to Saint Peter's Basilica and Saint John Lateran for their ceremonial usage.

☙

Legend has it that Cecilia's body, upon being exhumed in the San Callisto catacombs in 1599 by Cardinal Sfondsato for the upcoming Jubilee Year, was found to be incorruptible, complete even with congealed blood still on her neck. She is in fact the earliest uncorrupted saint on record.

There were apparently many witnesses to this miraculous occurrence, including Stefano Maderno, who later sculpted a magnificent image of her body based on what he had seen—though, since her body was actually in a small coffin, there was no way her body could have been positioned on its side like it is in the sculpture. Though the Catholic Church used to declare an incorruptible corpse as a sign of a saint's holiness, today it no longer does so, as there may be scientific reasons why the body has remained in the state it is in.

The statue has her holding out, apparently as she was found, three fingers on one hand and one on another, a sign of her belief in the Trinity: the three in one and the one in three.

The charged atmosphere of Cecilia's death and her eventual role as an idealized image of purity in the Church throughout history has more recently been portrayed, with stunning effect, by the African American artist Kehinde Wiley, who did the official portrait of President Barack Obama, in his painting *The Virgin Martyr Saint Cecilia* (2008). In his version, a young black woman is rendered a martyr to the racial injustices of the United States—a powerful reminder that the politics of martyrdom have not left our world, but have, if anything, gained traction in different contexts.

☙

Martyrdom, because self-grounding as a concept, easily becomes a platform for the idealization of purity and holiness, giving us a pathway by which

The Idol of Purity

to understand the significance of young, female, virgin martyrs within the history of the church. Seeing only the goodness within the person, their saintly aura that is bestowed upon them as such, is symbolically aligned with the purity of the untainted, the virginal, and the feminine.

The many hagiographical accounts of the Roman virgin martyrs make these connotations abundantly clear. They represent the ideal of what a self-grounding faith, a self-founding love, should be: blind to reality in order to posit the self in love as the loving self.

Though such a configuration can be as delusional as any other fantasy, it is also the structural necessity for an established sense of self, as well as any lasting, loving relationship. We idealize in order to maintain our sense of self, as well as our sense of the other, even if our views deviate from the reality before us. This is a tendency well-documented psychologically, and captured, one might argue, at the heart of all religious desire.

Though we may deny the historical accuracy of the miraculous lives of the saints, or the biblical narratives upon which many of those lives are modeled, it is impossible to discard completely the structure of idealization altogether. Indeed we, as a human race, would be significantly impoverished should we seek to live without this capacity in us.

This truth is what I keep before me as I glance up at the ceiling in the church of Sant'Agnese fuori le mura, noting how Saints Agnus and Cecilia, despite their youth and innocence, appear in idealized imagery in order to inspire the devout who make the pilgrimage here on the margins of the city.

The pilgrims who visit this church and its grounds are like the early Christians who sought to be buried in the catacombs underneath the church. To reside for eternity in close proximity to this young martyr was to touch the source of one's faith, to be likewise placed along the vertical axis to heaven that shot straight up from her tomb to the altar in the sanctuary above. Agnes was one's very access to this divine ascent.

The force of an idealization is no negligible act. Agnes and Cecilia inspired others because they gave them a voice, a route to selfhood in an empire that actually denied political and practical selfhood to many. Martyrdom was the means by which many secured a voice against their oppressors. To the sovereign claims of the Roman Empire come the sovereign claims of the young women who would assert their own right to self-governance. The competing claims for autonomy and the right to self-determinacy were at the heart of these martyr's acts, and they are as legitimate in this sense now as they were then.

One need only glance for a moment at Wiley's painting to comprehend the contemporary significance of Cecilia's original actions in refusing to go along with the marriage she was forced into. What Wiley has done is make clearer the implications of martyrdom from a perspective that was seemingly lost to history when the post-Constantinian church became immersed in imperial power and eventual global, colonialist expansion: when not used to legitimate sovereign power, martyrdom has the potential to give a voice to the voiceless, to inspire justice in our world and to bring the powers that be to accountability.

Buried beneath the layers of history and an all-male hierarchy lies the story of a young woman forced into an impossible situation and looking for a means of escape as her salvation. What we have in the hagiographic events of her life will undoubtedly never match the actual events of her life and death. But we can see now more clearly than ever what a recovered narrative might more closely resemble: the vision of Wiley's painting captures this more accurately than any of us could put into words.

Fabricating Yet Finding Sacrality

He focuses on the church of Santa Prassede where many dubious relics are located—Among these relics are those of Saints Valentine and Zeno, Prassede and Pudentiana—The pillar associated with Christ's death—He describes how ahistorical stories of saints go hand in hand with the creation of churches and the practice of faith

VERMEER'S PAINTING OF SAINT Praxidis (1655) tells the entire story of another young martyr. She was devoted to those willing to sacrifice their lives for the faith, so devoted that she was said to gather up their precious blood with a sponge and store it in a jar. This relic of the martyrs tells us how important their lives, and deaths, are to the church. The church built in her honor in Rome fittingly became a reliquary for the bones of the saints and martyrs of Rome, many of whom were moved here from the catacombs on the outskirts of town.

Focused on Saint Praxedes (or Praxidis), this church was built in the eighth to ninth centuries, and is an architectural collage of older Roman forms. It was originally part of a Byzantine monastery that was built to house monks fleeing the iconoclast controversy in the East. It is supposed to be a titular church, hence built on the site of a house church, but this is now known to not be true. Therefore it memorializes the original idea of a titular church though it is not itself one.

༄

Santa Prassede was built by Pope Paschal I, who also built S. Maria in Trastevere, and it was constructed as a repository for relics that were being frequently looted by pilgrims coming to Rome at this time. We should keep in mind that this was a period in history when the catacombs were closed down and subsequently forgotten until the nineteenth century.

There are reportedly 2,300 martyrs' relics that were eventually moved here. The alleged relics of Prassede and Pudentiana are located in the *confessio*, including a sponge they are said to have used to collect the blood of martyrs. There is a statue in the back of Prassede squeezing blood into a vase, located near her "bed," which is nothing more than a black stone slab.

Historical record tells us, however, that these stories are all unsubstantiated and that these saints might not have even existed. There may even just have been a lady with one of these names who simply donated the land for the church.

If we today call martyrdom into question as an act of grounding what cannot be grounded, we should not be surprised that many early saints, who supposedly did just this, were themselves fabrications for the faith.

ക

There is here moreover a Chapel of Saint Zeno, with his relics enshrined, and the chapel itself completely covered in mosaics (also from the ninth century). In general, historians have no idea who this saint was, but he is often referred to as a companion of St. Valentine, who was himself taken off the official list of saints in the twentieth century, as his existence is now in doubt as well.

The chapel was built to resemble a cubiculum, or a small room in the catacombs. It was originally intended to be a tomb for the mother of Pope Paschal I, Theodora. Interestingly, there is an inscription that reads "Episcopa Theodora," which translates as "Bishop Theodora," a point taken up frequently by those seeking the ordination of women as priests in the Catholic Church. The title, however, has been used throughout history to refer to the wives of bishops, as clergy were sometimes married in the early Church.

St. Valentine of Rome, for his part, was allegedly an early Roman martyr who was killed on the Via Flaminia near the Ponte Milvio, north of Rome. Many legends surround him, often stating that he was a Roman priest who performed miracles as well as secret weddings for Christian couples, and that he refused to deny his faith and so was eventually put to death for his beliefs.

Fabricating Yet Finding Sacrality

The relationship of Saint Valentine to Saint Zeno—perhaps a martyr himself, or perhaps the bishop of Verona—is unclear, though it is depicted in mosaics in the church. Valentine died on February 14, 269, hence the feast day celebrating his death is recognized as "Valentine's Day," which began being celebrated in 496. His relics were kept in San Valentino in Rome until they were moved to Santa Prassede by Pope Nicholas IV in the thirteenth century. His association with romantic love appears to stem from the time period surrounding Geoffrey Chaucer's *Parlement of Foules* (fourteenth century), a poem on the nature of love and free will.

The Chapel of the Pillar, which is said to contain the pillar that Christ was tied to while being flogged, is controversial in and of itself. The pillar was brought back from the holy land in the thirteenth century, though other legends claim that Saint Helena also might have brought it back with her in the fourth century. It is nonetheless still venerated as a holy relic associated with Christ's death. Experts today tell us, however, that this relic most likely originated in the fifth century in Jerusalem and that it could not be the real pillar, as it is too ornate and not from the right era.[1]

If one leaves the church of Santa Prassede confused about the nature of relics and their authenticity, they would not be alone.

Perhaps the inclusion of so many potentially false relics is indicative of the Church's intentions at the time, which were to reassert the superiority of Roman traditions and practices since the Byzantine ones had dominated the churches in Rome for the past century or so (including the strong influence of mosaics in Rome's ecclesial art). This church in particular was built to house relics for pilgrims coming to Rome, and thereby to illustrate a particularly Roman ethos.[2]

Though it would be fairly easy to miss the church when touring the city today, various saints throughout the years did not miss its significance. A swath of stories seems to indicate too that the presence of God moves uniquely through these relics and through the church itself. Saint Bridget of Sweden (fourteenth century) claimed that the painted crucifix of Christ

---

1. The pillar itself was only moved to this chapel in the twentieth century as women were previously not allowed to touch it because a menstruating woman might render holy things unclean.

2. Duffy, *Saints and Sinners*, 99.

once spoke to her in the chapel to the right of the main altar. St. Charles Borromeo (sixteenth century), a significant counter-Reformation figure in the Catholic Church, used to spend whole nights praying in the *confessio* under the altar where the relics were housed. There is even a chair kept in a side chapel that once belonged to him, attesting to his presence there to this day.

※

It may obscure matters to announce that historians today tell us that Prassede may not have been a real person, that the pillar of Christ in another chapel here is not authentic, that another chapel's namesake, St. Zeno, probably didn't exist, and his companion, St. Valentine, most likely didn't exist either. But none of this seems to deter pilgrims from coming here to stand before the pillar and pray. Likewise, none of this seemed to alter the faith of Charles Borromeo or Bridget of Sweden.

I am reminded, when I think of these things, how St. Ignatius of Loyola himself held his first mass in the basilica of Maria Maggiore in Rome, in front of a dubious relic—the crib of the infant Jesus—or how he used to pray on Janiculum Hill in the Tempietto of Bramante where it was wrongly believed, according to an alternative legend, that Peter had been crucified upside down.

※

To journey to these places, however, speaks not just of their "original" meaning, but of the subsequent saints who brought their interior worlds to life there.[3]

3. The Church of St. Peter in Montorio (Chiesa di San Pietro in Montorio) is set on the Janiculum Hill on your way down toward Trastevere. It commemorates the site where Peter was said, according to some legends, to have been crucified. The church itself dates from the fifth century. Built on the site of a Benedictine abbey with Byzantine influence, the Tempietto was sponsored by Ferdinand and Isabella of Spain in 1502 and it was completed in 1512. This is why, to this day, to access the Tempietto, you have to go through the Spanish Embassy. It was designed by Donato Bramante, and has become a model for Renaissance Italian architecture. The "Temple of Bramante," or "Tempietto" ("little temple") is a premier example of Renaissance architecture and is a small shrine dedicated to the martyrdom of St. Peter. Like Bernini's baldacchino, the Tempietto is a piece of art (sculpture). The Tempietto was supposedly the site where Peter was crucified, but we

Fabricating Yet Finding Sacrality

To hear these mistaken facts as a refutation of faith, or as what might block a potential epiphany, is to miss the point, and to misunderstand the nature of revelation—a problem encountered today as when reading the fantastic tales of Scripture, just as when casting about for the most historically accurate religious sites.

Revelation, in this sense, is not necessarily a miraculously hand-delivered moment of divine speech. It is what accompanies a genuine encounter with that which lies beyond us, and which we find frequently in those moments of silence and relationship that speak volumes without having to utter an intelligible word to us.

I come to this church, as I come to all of the churches of Rome, eager to receive a revelation, an insight so brilliant and insightful that I find myself dislocated from my normal routines and bound by a heightened awareness to circumstances both within and without that are completely beyond my control.

I have come to believe that spaces reserved for such moments, spaces that devote every inch of themselves to receiving such depth and transcendence, become sacred to us through their ability to direct and contain the encounters we are searching for. The presence or absence of ostensibly false or dubious relics says very little about what else is possible in such locations, and I take this consideration to heart when I ease my own burdens within their confines.

---

now know that he was actually killed in the Circus of Nero, where St. Peter's Basilica is located today. When St. Ignatius was elected as the first Superior General of the Jesuits in 1541, he spent three days here deciding whether to accept the post (in the end, he did).

Epiphany

He affirms that the pilgrim may be struck by an epiphany while listening for what comes from beyond the ordinary—He shows how revelation appears only with one's openness and receptivity—He recalls previous visits to St. Stephen's Cathedral in Vienna, the Cathedral Church of St. Peter in Cologne, and St. Bavo's Cathedral in Ghent—These churches, he reflects, seemed to unlock something within him that he had previously been unaware of—He concludes that only when one is able to accept the darkness within, can they accept the darkness of humanity

WHAT IS REVEALED TO the pilgrim is received on a different register than we are normally accustomed to, though the planes of the pilgrim's world and the everyday touch and even collide at times.

An epiphany may strike the pilgrim because the pilgrim, like the mystic, listens for what comes from beyond the ordinary. To be able to recognize the journey of life for what it is, a pathway quickly traversed between birth and death, allows the pilgrim to focus on what really matters, what remains when the extraneous is removed.

There is certainly something of the ascetic in this suggestion, a stance counter to the world that grants one insight through their elevation above it all. There is also a poverty that is embraced as essential for making the journey, a letting go that quickens the mind and the spirit. This letting go is what has been traditionally identified with penitence, and the cultivation of a humility that refuses to transition into pride.

☙

The moral reformation of the self that takes place internally for the pilgrim transforms the entire self so that living in the world becomes entirely different. Henceforth, the pilgrim inhabits the uninhabitable, a liminal space that invites the revealing of things unknown, unseen, wholly beyond the ordinary. At times it may appear as simply a shift in perspective, an awareness of a presence or absence, the feeling of belonging, a therapeutic healing, a resolution of past hurt, the mark of time's passing, or any number of things that all bear the gravity of an event.

The epiphany, perhaps as saints like Bridget once experienced it, is to allow these small changes to override the self, to let them merge with the self, so that the self can be remade, reborn, untethered to the static realities that ossify all around it.

Our capacity to be human demands nothing less than a creative reimagining of reality and an ability to see far beyond all the economies and relations that seem otherwise unchanging and stagnant in our world.

༄

Revelation appears because one is ready for it. It appears because one is open to receiving it. It is the openness itself that actually brings about the revelation, as odd as this proposition might seem.

This oddness is, in turn, its uncanny and mysterious nature. Without the capacity to welcome and embrace, without the hospitality that brings the foreign and the different into one's home, there is no revelation. It is in this way that we come to realize that it is only by becoming a pilgrim that we can receive those words meant only for us, even if there is no divine hand guiding them to us.

Our openness and receptivity are what shape the message and sort through the noise so that we are able to hear only what it is that we needed to hear, and, in that sense, what was meant for us.

That religion has a means, an entire language, to describe this process, should come as no surprise. It is one well worth listening to and learning from. If those of us who have left organized religion are to hear the words that can transform us, that can even convert our souls to whatever purpose or community, then we will need to revisit and rediscover those mediums for epiphany, the churches and myriad other holy sites the world over, that continue to speak to humanity still.

༄

Sacred Pilgrim, Secular Pilgrim

It is important to notice the way that walking demonstrates a subconsciousness that is central to the processes of pilgrimage. Being open to the pilgrimage itself means being open to oneself, allowing all that one faces to become part of oneself at the same time that one lets everything within escape into the light of day.

There are moments where the light from a farmer's field, or a soft light let in through a church window, merges seamlessly with something arising from deep within, a feeling, a trauma, a sense of remorse or loss, a loneliness that follows you constantly, any number of things that you have released into the atmosphere and that could only surface if you give them the space in which to do so.

⁂

When I first walked into St. Stephen's Cathedral in Vienna, or the Cathedral Church of St. Peter in Cologne, or St. Bavo's Cathedral in Ghent, each of these spaces seems to unlock something within me that I had previously been unaware of, that I had not allowed to surface before those moments. I am confronted with the deepest of personal insights about who I was and about the choices I had made in life because I allow myself to be open to them, at those times, in those places.

This unlocking, which takes place when it decides to do so and not as calculated beforehand, is precisely what happens when we move against the currents of the world and allow ourselves to yield to the subconscious flows moving entirely with a will of their own. By allowing these processes to unfold we expose layers of ourselves, layers of our history and life story, allowing them to encounter the layers of others, other stories and other traditions.

⁂

I walk the streets of Rome asking the history that juts up from the underground, the centuries of turmoil and pain, to speak to my own turmoil and pain, to lessen the grief I might bear, to assist me in letting go of the burdens I shoulder. The large wooden confessionals exist in cathedrals for just this reason. It is in these rich juxtapositions of a shared history and the individual life that the most creative work on one's soul takes place.

Epiphany

Accepting the darkness of humanity can only be achieved insofar as we are able to accept the darkness within ourselves. This truth is not something the pilgrim sets out to accomplish so much as it is the way that the pilgrim must take to enter more fully into the pilgrimage. To ignore this dynamic is to cease being a pilgrim altogether.

The Politics of Memory

He mentions the history of Santa Maria in Trastevere—The politics of memory—What is preserved and what is repressed—He notices the juxtaposition of Mary as bearer of God and the rehabilitated image of a kidnapper and rapist Roberto Altemps—He explains that this juxtaposition is a sign of the tensions caused by the fusion of the spiritual and the material—The difficulty and biases of historical memory

SANTA MARIA IN TRASTEVERE was originally a fourth-century church that was restored in the twelfth and nineteenth centuries. It was one of the original tituli, or *domus ecclesia*, before the current basilica's construction had begun. Allegedly this was the first church in Rome where mass was openly celebrated. The church may, arguably, also be the first church in the world dedicated to Mary—a significant honor in the Catholic world.

The building itself is a collage of Roman and Christian forms. Random Roman imperial columns are inside, the tower is Romanesque, the mosaics date from the twelfth century, the portico dates from the seventeenth century, the doors are reused Roman ones, ancient Christian inscriptions line the walls in the portico (put there in the nineteenth century in a hasty archaeological touch; some were in fact tombstones taken off the Via Appia), the floor is medieval, and the ceiling is from the seventeenth century.

There are twenty-two pillars in total within the church, each taken from a different ancient Roman ruin, or more likely from Egypt as spoils of war. The church was in fact designed to fit the columns. Pillars in the nave originally had pagan gods on them: Isis, Serapis, and Harpocrates. After their identities were discovered in the nineteenth century, however, their images were removed and destroyed.

The Politics of Memory

The memory of the anti-pope Anacletus II, once the titular cardinal here, was effaced from this church by Pope Innocent II (d. 1143). This act was a *damnatio memoriae*, a "damning of memory," and it was commonly practiced when one pope's claims eventually overtook those of another, who was only subsequently labeled as an "anti-pope." It is important to remember that when there were periods of time with more than one pope, the Church was more or less divided, with large numbers of supporters for both popes.

Anacletus, who was apparently descended from a Jewish convert, had ruled as pope until his death in Rome (d. 1138), but then was declared to be an anti-pope at the Second Lateran council in order to unite a divided global church.[1] Pope Innocent II himself, who was from the Roman region of Trastevere, where this church is located, is buried here in a porphyry sarcophagus that had originally belonged to the Roman Emperor Hadrian and was kept at the Castel Sant'Angelo.[2] This was a symbol of the papal office coming more and more to resemble a monarchy. Similarly, Pope Anastasius, the next pope, was buried in a sarcophagus that was intended for Saint Helena, Constantine's mother, which is now on prominent display in the Vatican museums.

※

The politics of memory—what is preserved and what is repressed—are not only on display in the battles waged between popes, or between competing cultural representations on display in the church (Egyptian, Roman, Christian), but also in another, more notorious story layered within the Church's history.

The tomb of Roberto Altemps (d. 1586) is just to the side of the main altar. He was the son of a cardinal. He was executed for adultery (but not kidnapping and rape, which is what he actually did), rather than simply be forced to marry the woman he had raped (as was commonly practiced) since he was already married. Pope Sixtus V had him beheaded as a sign that even those among the nobility are subject to Church law.

An inscription below his bust in the sanctuary simply says that he was "extinguished before his time." The choice to portray him as an innocent-looking child, however, as is clear from first glance upon his beautiful

---

1. Duffy, *Saints and Sinners*, 141.
2. Duffy, *Saints and Sinners*, 139.

marble bust, was no doubt an effort to rehabilitate his image after his death. The reason he is buried here is no doubt directly related to the fact that the side chapel, Cappella Altemps, was paid for by his family.

There is more than a little irony in the fact that the chapel paid for by his family contains one of the oldest icons of Mary (c. sixth to ninth centuries), *Madonna della Clemenza* (Our Lady of Mercy). She is depicted as a Roman empress and the presence of this icon may be the reason that the Church was eventually dedicated to Mary. The juxtaposition of Mary as Theotokos, or bearer of God, and the tomb of Roberto Altemps is striking, as well as reminiscent of various (heretical) theological speculations that Mary conceived a child due to an undisclosed rape—something she would have felt shame over, if indeed this was the case, and so did not reveal as the nature of her pregnancy. This is not the Church's teaching, and it of course amounts to no more than speculation, but it has been a claim doggedly following Mary's pregnancy for centuries.

Whenever I have taken students to this church in the past and pointed out this glaring juxtaposition between the rehabilitated image of a kidnapper and rapist and the ever-pure, ever-virgin Mother of God, it never fails to anger nearly every one of my students. How the Church today refuses to acknowledge or deal with this tension is merely another level of frustration regarding the treatment of women and the violence of men within the Church as a whole.

Perhaps the messiness of this awful tension speaks to the Catholic willingness to embrace the embodied nature of human and divine existence. Life is not always neatly dealt with, and errors abound that we wish to see covered over or eradicated altogether. But, as in many Catholic churches, the tensions are nonetheless scattered throughout.

The inevitable and inseparable fusion of the spiritual and the material takes place when I look at the icon of Mary in the Cappella Altemps. The icon is so old that it appears as worn and frayed, having lost a good deal of its color and realistic appearance. Nonetheless when I see it, I am reminded of how icons are said to be "written" and not "painted." One writes an icon like one writes Scripture, recognizing somehow that words are already images and that our ideas are already embodied.

The Politics of Memory

It is in this sense that, as I stroll later that same evening through the Piazza del Popolo, I wish I could write the sun going down slowly over the square, wish I could write the lover's embrace halfway across its cobblestone floor, wish I could write the light sway of green at the base of the Villa Borghese or the sounds of silverware and plates being cleared from a table only a stone's throw behind me on the sidewalk.

My desire to capture the simplest of daily realities as themselves bearing an iconic representation of a sacred nature stems from my inability to separate the ordinary from the extraordinary, the natural from the supernatural, and the material from the spiritual. Presences of various kinds overlap and permeate each other, in ways that beg for our understanding while permanently evading it at the same time.

I am reminded of this fusion of materiality and spirituality the next morning when I walk into a church in Rome dedicated to the stigmata of Saint Francis of Assisi, and so not just to the saint himself, but specifically to the marks of Christ's death that he miraculously bore on his own body.

In a country so devoted to the supernatural marks of one's devotion to Jesus and his suffering, it is no surprise that such a church exists. The more recently arisen cult surrounding the Franciscan saint Padre Pio is likewise enough testimony to the esteem that Catholics hold for those who bear the signs of Christ's wounds in imitation of his life. To follow Jesus so closely as to bear his sufferings with him is, for many, the ultimate sign of one's faith.

These are reminders of how the bodily and the spiritual cannot be separated from one another, much as the Catholic focus on transubstantiation signals as well.

As a painting of Saint Catherine of Siena in S. Sabina also details through her rejection of a heavenly crown in favor of the crown of thorns and the reality of suffering in this world, there is much to be learned about the Catholic saintly ideal from such focal points in its history. The material nature of suffering and the embodiments of faith collide and coalesce in such geographical spaces.

Though I do not wish to see suffering itself idealized and so sought out as a religious asceticism without purpose, there is much to be gleaned from the linkage between an acceptance of one's suffering and an embrace of the complexities of our embodied lives.

Displays of Power

He reflects on San Giovanni in Laterano, Rome's first true Christian basilica—A historical site of the papal residences—He explains the overlap of the spiritual and the political in the basilica—For him, a great deal is possible in terms of reaching the "highest heights" and "lowest lows" within such sacred spaces

THE CONTRADICTIONS AND COMPLEXITY do not relent for a moment as I walk throughout the city. The layers of history and devotion only seem to add more questioning in equal proportion to wonder. But what am I to make of the expansiveness of papal authority and glory that resides within one of the largest monuments to sovereignty in the Christian world?

San Giovanni in Laterano represents the splendor of papal power, its glory and majesty, while also maintaining its history of decay and corruption. Built by Constantine shortly after he converted to Christianity to be the "mother of all churches" throughout the world, the Lateran, as it is sometimes called, became a papal palace, a sign of greatness and the Church's sovereign rule—something the sheer size of its imposing façade today certainly reflects. Though it was left to fall into ruin during the relocation of the papacy to Avignon, France in the fourteenth century, its subsequent rebuilding was an imperative undertaking as a sign of the restoration of papal power.

ஃ

The wide boulevards that can be seen to link the major basilicas today were actually created by Pope Sixtus V, who leveled numerous buildings in order to make this possible. This destruction was brought about to demonstrate the majesty of these buildings and of papal authority, but also so as to make things easier for pilgrims visiting Rome.

A rather authoritarian gesture, it was repeated by Mussolini in the twentieth century when he cleared a path running from Saint Peter's to the Tiber River—what is today the Via della Conciliazione—in order, it was said, to impress Hitler upon the latter's visit to Rome in 1938.[1]

It would be an accurate description of things to say that today's Rome is very much Mussolini's vision of it in many ways.[2] This should be no great shock, for Catholicism itself historically favored monarchical governance and was extremely opposed to democratic political forms up until the late eighteenth century, when Napoleon invaded Italy and brought about a rethinking of Catholicism's relationship to democratic systems (basically the Church's attempt to curry favor with Napoleon, which included the historical "discovery" of a Saint Napoleon whom no one could quite exactly recall as a living historical figure).[3]

Simply entering the Lateran is enough to recall the paradoxes of power residing within the Catholic Church. Humility and humanity are both equally on display and the temptation to shove such tensions to the side in order to simply be overwhelmed by the expansiveness of the church, as if it were a museum like any other, is equally overwhelming. But these tensions cannot be hidden and, if anything, are becoming more and more visible among the ruins of what the Catholic Church has become compared to its former prestige and influence.

There is a good deal of controversy surrounding the relationships of popes and dictators throughout history, from medieval monarchs to twentieth-century totalitarian and fascist leaders.

Pope Pius XII, as pope during the Second World War, is often accused of not doing or saying enough to denounce Hitler's rise to power and his

1. Hughes, *Rome*, 246, 430.
2. Kneale, *Rome*, 277–359.
3. Duffy, *Saints and Sinners*, 259.

genocidal aims. Critics are quick to point out that he was the papal legate to Germany prior to his election, while supporters point out that he did suggest in numerous contexts, and in a radio address, specific criticisms of Nazism, even going so far as to secretly support Jewish refugees in Rome.[4] He even left Rome when Hitler visited Mussolini because, it was said, he could not stand the sight of the man.

What is not often discussed is how his efforts to remain neutral and to sign a Concordat with Hitler in 1933 were actions mirroring that of Pope Benedict XV during the First World War, who strove to remain above the fray of political involvement.[5] Nazism was also perceived by many at the time as the "last bulwark" against godless communism and so was indirectly supported at times within the Catholic Church, especially in Germany, as a necessary countermeasure.

It is certainly also the case that popes Pius XI and Pius XII were not fans of either liberalism or democracy, opinions we have seen held by popes time and again.[6] Nonetheless, Pius XII's reputation was damaged tremendously by his indecision and by not directly denouncing the deportation of Jews. He claimed it would have done no good and would only have risked the safety of Catholics everywhere, but a lot of people see cowardice in such actions taken to protect only his own people.

It is certainly the case that many Catholic networks after WWII helped to hide and move former Nazi war criminals throughout the world, a stain that still lingers upon the Church.

For his part, Pius XII's final days were characterized by trying to censor liberal theologies and theologians from spreading their views within the Church, as well as the Worker Priest movement, which sought solidarity with trade unions, but was seen as too radical and too close to communism. These fears would re-emerge years later in the pontificate of John Paul II (and his right-hand man, Joseph Ratzinger, the eventual Pope Benedict

---

4. Duffy, *Saints and Sinners*, 347.
5. Duffy, *Saints and Sinners*, 333, 347.
6. Duffy, *Saints and Sinners*, 344.

XVI) in the condemnations of certain liberation theologians from a variety of Third World contexts.[7]

☙

San Giovanni in Laterano is Rome's first Christian basilica, built by Constantine in the fourth century. It was originally built in open country, with fields surrounding it on all sides. It has been (partially) destroyed by fire (in 1308 and 1360), earthquake, and neglect, but was subsequently rebuilt several times throughout history. It was sacked by barbarians too (for example, the Visigoths in 450 and the Vandals in 455). Nonetheless, mass was first celebrated here on November 9, 318, making this the first actual, "freestanding" church in Rome, at least as we think of what churches look like today.

Originally called the Basilica Constantiniana, it was named Saint John Lateran for Saints John the Baptist and John the Evangelist by Pope Lucius in 1144. The title "Lateran" however comes from Laterani, the name of the family who originally owned the property.

Opting for this combined name was a clever way to put the Romans at ease about this new Christian religion and the gigantic building it spawned, as its presence did not erase a more Roman heritage underneath. It also appears that Constantine may have desired to build it in order to replace a military barracks governed by one of his early competitors for power in Rome (Maxentius), and so cared more about replacing his rivals' works with "new" sites than about promulgating Christianity, as he sponsored new building projects, not the continuation of ones that Christians had already begun.[8] This context would go some ways toward explaining why rebuilding St. Peter's basilica was not undertaken until much later in history.

☙

Essentially, the church was built to commemorate Constantine's victory over his rival, the Emperor Maxentius, in 312, when he saw a sign (the Chi-Rho) and a voice that said "In this sign, you shall conquer." Many historians have subsequently questioned whether or not Constantine merely

---

7. Duffy, *Saints and Sinners*, 372.
8. Rüpke, *Pantheon*, 374.

used Christianity as a political maneuver in order to gain advantage over his rivals.

Constantine's conversion also did not mean that Roman gods ceased to be worshipped—as such religious practices clearly continued. It rather meant that Christians were free to worship their God as other religions had done. From this point onward as well, Christians received official funding and support from the empire, which was mainly in the form of tax exemption (a practice that still continues today).

The Church was therefore, over time, able exploit this relationship in order to slowly eradicate Roman religious influence, denounced as "paganism" and "idolatry" from a Christian point of view, and to gain an impressive foothold within European political and administrative positions.

The grandeur and majesty of the architecture and universal scope of Roman churches automatically invokes the sovereign claims of the Catholic Church, which developed over centuries to justify its dominance over peoples and places that it deemed subject to its power. To breathe in the atmosphere within Rome's largest basilicas is to become its subject, to feel its weight press upon you, making clear your place within a constructed hierarchical order that encompasses all of creation and the uncreated alike—from the heavens to the taxonomies of all living things.

Faith, for so many people today, is an exercise in constructing oneself *as* sovereign over oneself and one's life. Our inability to control various facets of our lives causes us to seek a sort of refuge in a religion's ability to grant an individual a strong sense of identity—meaning and purpose—through the sovereign gestures of its God in relation to the individual who links their existence to their God's. To say "I believe" can be a way for some to call themselves into existence and to create a foundation upon a ground that is otherwise unjustifiable.

I walk through the glorious cathedrals of Rome contemplating the loss of my sovereign self, its dissolution in the face of life's many contingencies—those moments of suffering and loss that take away the strong sense of self that otherwise accompanies us all at times. Atheism, from this point of view, can be for some little more than a recognition that the ground underneath their feet is not as solid as they had once imagined it to be.

Sacred Pilgrim, Secular Pilgrim

Divorce, for me, was only a reminder that those aspects of life that feel so secure at times can also be the source of our greatest disillusionments, that what I had thought would give me a daily strength could become a constant and profound weakness. The scars I bear from this wound are still carried by me, in ways that even feel physically borne.

⁂

The Lateran Palace, for its part, was the official papal residence from 501 until 1309 (until the Avignon papacy, which relocated for a time to France), and up until 1870 all popes were crowned here. This particular church is actually the main cathedral of the diocese of Rome. It is the "mother of all churches" and so also the most elevated of them all. Printed twice on the façade is the inscription *Omnium Urbis et orbis ecclesiarum mater et caput* ("The mother and head of all churches of the city and of the world").

Technically speaking, then, this is the major cathedral of Rome, *not* St. Peter's, though St. Peter's has become known, practically speaking, as the primary basilica in Rome. The area just below Saint John Lateran's apse contains the Papal Throne, however, which is located there and not at St. Peter's. This is the *cathedra*, or chair, from which the pope can declare a doctrine as infallible. The very presence of such a throne certainly recalls the glory that surrounds monarchies, and the highly visible, empty throne is a familiar image of power in cathedrals around the world.

Beyond these details, and distinctly noticeable as soon as one enters the building, enormous statues of the twelve apostles are evenly spaced within the basilica's nave, including Simon Peter, Andrew (Peter's brother), James and John ("sons of Zebedee"), Philip, Thaddeus ("Jude"), Bartholomew, Thomas, James ("the lesser"), Matthew (Levi), Simon, and Judas Iscariot (later replaced by Matthias after Judas's death by suicide). Such artworks functioned like stained glass in later cathedrals, as they served to explain the lives of these saints pictorially, often including symbols of their martyrdoms and illuminating central biblical stories at the same time.

⁂

Pope Innocent III (d. 1216) is also buried in Saint John Lateran. One of the most powerful medieval popes, he oversaw the Fourth Lateran Council, declared the Magna Carta "null and void," launched new crusades, established the doctrine of transubstantiation, and required Christians to go to confession and communion at least once a year.[9] He tried his best to enforce orthodoxy and eliminate heresy, even going so far as to grant crusading indulgences to those who fought against the Cathar and Albigensian heresies. These "apostolic" poverty movements were deeply influential at this point in history as a reaction against the corruptions of the Catholic Church, and many would identify them as precursors to the eventual revolutionary impulses of the Reformation.

It was during this time as well that Saint Francis of Assisi, providing something of a counterpoint to such acts of power, became active and founded the Franciscan order, which Pope Innocent actually accepted as a legitimate order in the end, though their vows of extreme poverty and the renunciation of property and possession were to create major headaches for the Church on the whole.[10] Innocent's zeal for eliminating heretics was continued by Pope Gregory IX, who turned the Inquisition over to the Dominican friars and made it part of canon law that heretics should be burned at the stake by secular powers.[11]

I often think about these impulses for reform and the desire to embrace a life of poverty as they are both motives manifested in tension with the institutional Church throughout history. The way that these tensions continuously move throughout the body of the faithful parallels the tension that permanently resides between the pilgrim and the tourist.

We strive for purity and we need to make space for clarity and calmness, though we are tempted by the structures of our world to relapse into the comfortable patterns and habits that we also need and adhere to. This tension is as inevitable as it is in constant need of balancing, for it cannot be eradicated altogether.

---

9. Duffy, *Saints and Sinners*, 148.
10. Duffy, *Saints and Sinners*, 150.
11. Duffy, *Saints and Sinners*, 152.

There are many halls of power within the Church, as much today as in the past, and the Lateran was once the seat of such political maneuvers, and on multiple levels. The very significant Lateran councils were held here, starting in 1123 and going until 1512.

These councils were really where the power of the cardinals began to be exercised together in community, giving a power to synods and councils that would eventually rival, and even challenge, papal power.[12] A Conciliarist movement calling for communal decision-making at the highest level is still active within the Church today, and it symbolizes an unresolved tension with the pope's unilateral power that may never be decided once and for all.

It used to be only gods and emperors, heroes and philosophers, who had statues so large created in their image, but the sculptures of the apostles standing in San Giovanni in Laterano are as immense and imposing as any others one might find throughout the world. They appear as if they might be Roman generals about to head into war, if not for the flowing robes and symbols of their martyrdoms held in their hands.

I have long wondered whether figures associated with poverty, the renunciation of earthly glory and a willingness to welcome their deaths for their faith, need to be immortalized with an ancient form of sculpture that tends to idealize the body in its quest for perfection. To me, this is why John Lateran is mainly a Constantinian church, exalting a deified emperor and an imperial, hierarchical Church.

As I stroll through the sanctuary on this particularly sunny day, a group of school children receives a lecture on the art and history of the building from a tour guide, while tourists meander throughout the sanctuary taking photos and the faithful sit quietly in adoration in a small side chapel. This site, as a whole, is in many ways a modern agora for the global tensions that accompany every spirituality, every artistic legacy, and every contested history. That all of this carries on in the shadow of the pope's throne does not lessen the complications or diversity on display.

---

12. Duffy, *Saints and Sinners*, 130.

The ostensibly more fervent believers are across the street, climbing on their knees up the holy stairs—La Scala Sancta—that Christ, allegedly, once himself ascended. This ancient staircase, which is said to be the twenty-eight stairs Jesus walked up to Pontius Pilate's house, has become a minor pilgrimage site in its own right. The devout pray and climb on their knees, step by step, often with rosaries in hand, toward a room known as the Sancta Sanctorum, or the "holy of holies," once reserved only for popes, but now open to anyone who can pay a small fee.

The Scala Sancta were brought back from Jerusalem by Saint Helena, Constantine's mother. The original stairs are now covered with wood, with some windows installed to see through the covering (though they were recently uncovered for the first time in many years by Pope Francis). Though most likely an apocryphal tale meant to disparage his character, the Reformer Martin Luther was said by Catholics to have only made it halfway up the stairs on his knees during a Jubilee pilgrimage to Rome in 1510 before stopping and quitting it altogether—a supposed sign of his lack of true faith.

֍

The notion of a special room designated as the holy of holies goes back to an even older Jewish tradition in which only the high priest could enter a certain room within the temple once a year on the Day of Atonement, Yom Kippur. If the priest was not first purified of all his sins, he would, it was said, be killed instantly by the divine radiance that shone before him.

A rope was tied around the priest's waist just in case he died and had to be pulled out of the room by those not capable of standing directly before God's presence.

The fact that the Catholic Church has its own parallel tradition is very intriguing to say the least, especially as the Gospels record the fact that, upon Jesus' death, the curtain that separated the holy of holies from the rest of the temple was torn in half, exposing the entire world to the divine presence while also, from another perspective, profaning the most sacred space in the world according to Judaic teaching.

The Catholic Church's desire to recreate a sacred space as a Sancta Santorum most likely reflects a desire to reinscribe a form of restricted sacrality for political-sovereign reasons, to legitimate the pope's power, rather than follow Christ all the way in renouncing such forms of political theology.

As we stroll casually out the front doors of the Lateran, my friend Gábor suggests to me that it may be easier these days to reach moments of personal epiphany while reading certain texts—sacred or literary—than in trying to find God in churches so given over to tourists and a stagnant museum-like atmosphere. As soon as the words escape his lips, I feel both the truth of his comment for so many—one that Protestantism certainly shares—but also a sadness at the loss of possibility for feeling faith as a physical-material experience as well.

My experience has been that a great deal is possible in terms of reaching the "highest heights" and "lowest lows" within such sacralized spaces, as crowded and devoid of silence and decorum as they can be, though an intentional effort must be made to detach and unplug from those elements that would distract and deflect possibilities for encounter.

A quiet alcove or portico, an unobserved spot under a tree, the desire to turn inward by closing one's eyes in the midst of a crowd, the slowing of one's pace in a line—so many alternative possibilities appear when we lead our bodies in unusual and intentional ways.

And so I walked on, open to whatever form of the sacred might appear to me along the many streets of Rome as likewise within its many churches.

The Holy of Holies

He realizes that his own life at the moment reflects both absences and longings, he wanders looking for the feeling of being at home—He further focuses on the Lateran—He explains how the Church unknowingly created museum spaces as secularized versions of sacred places—How material, previously housed at the Lateran, was moved to the Vatican museums—He emphasizes the thin line between the museum and sacred spaces

It has long occurred to me that the nonbeliever should not be feared as a threat by a religion whose deity cried out about feeling the absence of God right before dying. If anything, Christianity should be a religion that is precisely more attuned to experiences of darkness and absence, the loss of meaning and how one wanders through life without finding a home.

I realize that my own life at the moment reflects the absences and longings that characterize the lost. I wander through life looking for the feeling of being at home in my own life, a feeling that may very well never appear. Whether my pilgrimage on this planet will henceforth involve the suspension of meaning and the search for purpose, I do not know and, most days, the ambiguity of not knowing where my fate is headed is a burden that overwhelms me and threatens to further destabilize what little bits of sanity I have left.

Perhaps this all sounds somewhat extreme to say, and I think to some degree it is. But when I picture the worn shoes of the pilgrim, the sunburn and hunger that mark the body, the distance kept from comfort and feeling at home so that the journey might reveal more inward depth, more truth, and more insight about the reality of the self and what lies beyond it, I am reminded that there is something happening beneath the surface of all that I see that shapes me in ways both known and unknown.

Sacred Pilgrim, Secular Pilgrim

I realize too that the pilgrim takes on an extreme existence, if only for a while, in order to see that which lies beyond their immediate reality. My pilgrimage is not finished, and I am called, by myself, by those I love, and by a spirit that lays deep within me, to complete the journey as best I can.

I am not ready to give up, and I am not yet able to lay down the burdens I carry.

※

I noticed only today that I have lost the appetite for desserts, for those sweet morsels that I typically relish when on vacation or at home. I suddenly feel as if they have no place in the life I am living right now, where my focus has shifted dramatically to my inner world. I want only to feast on the essence of life and to open myself through my hunger and the leanness of my frame as it calls out for something immaterial to nourish it.

I did not set out to change to a different diet; I merely listened to my desires and allowed my body to lead me for a while, as it moves toward others pastures to graze. I am suddenly reminded too of how physical this search for something beyond myself has become.

※

Near the Sancta Sanctorum is a chapel with a sixth-century icon over the altar of the Redeemer known as the *Acheropita* (which means "not painted by human hands"). It has near it the inscription "There is no holier place in the world than this." Expressing directly a "Christology from above," "unpainted icons" (*acheiropoietically*, or "made without hands") are said to be painted by God.[1] The icons not painted by human hands became symbols of sovereign power in the history of the Church, as one might expect, such as the Palladium, "the imperial protective sign of Byzantium."[2]

1. Sloterdijk, *Spheres, Volume 2*, 712.

2. As Sloterdijk continues, "[I]n 622, the Eastern Roman Emperor even took this picture with him on the campaign against the Persians, which was deemed a Holy War. According to the radical-epiphanist legend, the mysterious picture of Christ had come into existence through direct projection from heaven or, to use a modern expression, "theographically"—painted by God (or, even more commonly, "acheiropoietically," made without hands). This could only be imagined as a cluster of rays from the world above casting the *eidos* of Christ directly on a terrestrial canvas and materializing it there." Sloterdijk, *Spheres*, 712.

The Holy of Holies

A good deal can be said at this point about the relationship of Wunderkammers, or "cabinets of curiosity," and the relics within them that eventually led to the creation of the modern-day museum. Again, attesting to the inseparability of the material and the spiritual, the Church has unknowingly been at the forefront of creating museum spaces that are, in turn, simply secularized versions of sacred spaces.

It has been claimed that, among its relics, the Lateran contains the ark of the covenant, "the tablets of Moses, the rod of Aaron, a golden urn of manna, the tunic of the Virgin, various pieces of clothing worn by John the Baptist including his hair shirt, the five loaves and two fishes which fed the five thousand, and the table used at the Last Supper," as well as the "foreskin and umbilical cord of Christ"—though many might also dispute such grandiose claims.[3] A lot of material at the Vatican museums was originally housed here and only later transferred there by Pope John XXIII in the twentieth century.

The history of the Vatican museums themselves, however, dates back to Pope Pius VI, the last pope of the eighteenth century, who saw that pilgrims coming to Rome were blending with tourists who were coming to see the splendors of the city in general—a trend that accompanied an increasingly secular and supposedly "enlightened" world.[4] This was the time, after all, of the French Revolution and the beginnings of a much larger political project then taking place to secularize Europe.

We might speculate that the Vatican museums were part of a general plan to draw back interest and power back to the papacy and to Catholicism in general. The French Revolution was a great blow to the Catholic Church, wherein property was confiscated and religion was essentially removed from the government in favor of a secular agenda. Many poor clergy in fact supported the Revolution, since the ecclesial hierarchy and the monarchy it supported had become so detached through their wealth.

The line between the museum and the Church's designated sacred spaces is a thin one, often blurred and in need of redrawing from time to time. Simply walking the streets of Rome today, one is immediately aware that

---

3. Sumption, *Age of Pilgrimage*, 317.
4. Duffy, *Saints and Sinners*, 252.

these tensions are but reflections of so many others that permeate the atmosphere.

Like most of the old city, parts of Rome are overrun by crowds, tourists mostly, who collectively congest the sidewalks and risk the destruction of anything like a serene or sublime moment. It is when I sit on the periphery of such crowds that I feel the most intense longings for connection, encounter, and relationship, knowing too, however, that there is something powerful to be gained by allowing myself to sit in these moments and simply absorb whatever manifests itself to me.

I have to welcome these spaces where I realize all at once the feelings that have accumulated and layered themselves within me like sediment on the bottom of a river. There is nowhere else to go, nothing else to do. The current flows all around me at a pace I cannot control and I can only sit still in its midst and further unfold myself, giving myself over from time to time to its unyielding force.

Saint Peter's Basilica

He recalls the first time he visited Saint Peter's Square on his honeymoon years ago, longing for transcendence and connection in his marriage—He focuses on the figure of Peter as a figure of tensions—He feels the tension between belief and unbelief in his inner soul—He finds the mystery of faith through allowing the materiality of life to overwhelm and overtake the spirituality of his self—He realizes that his loss of belief is inseparable from his faith—He believes that only by allowing the dark interior to engulf and enrich him with its force, can he enter the brightness of the light

I prefer coming to the Saint Peter's Square after midnight, long after dinner and possibly one too many drinks, passing through it on my way to bed, stopping there for a moment and assessing myself, my life, as if this were a routine occurrence. Today the square is hot and crowded during the day and I sit under a few columns in the outstretched arms of Bernini's designs that border the square, resting in the shade before leaving to ascend Janiculum Hill right behind me.

This hill in particular has always drawn me into its orbit. There are far fewer people here and the views are more scenic. It is possible to lose myself on that hillside for hours uninterrupted, and for that reason, and for its beauty, I wander along its edges nearly every time I return to the city.

When I first encountered this massive basilica on my honeymoon decades ago, I was simply awed, the high ceilings and cold marble speaking to my inner longing for transcendence. I walked silently through its interior for over an hour, lost in a world of tranquility and placid emotion. I had wanted so badly to find God then, as I had also wanted so badly to feel connected in my marriage. Neither were able to fix a permanent hold on me.

For years I had conflated marriage with a sense of home, of being "at home" in my life, grounded and rooted. So many social structures, familial expectations, and religious connotations all led me to believe that being married would allow me to feel "at home" in my life, as if I had achieved one of the most significant things a human being could accomplish. Being married was the end goal—or vocation—toward which I had been journeying and its embrace would bring a sense of belonging I had only ever felt with my family of origin previously.

For a variety of reasons, mainly having to do with fundamental incompatabilities between us, I never felt grounded in my marriage—in fact the opposite was the case. My marriage became, from my perspective, an inverted pilgrimage without end, a liminal space of uneasiness that I constantly sought to ground, but to no avail. I was thrown back to a groundlessness that undid me rather than provide peace in the midst of life's uncertainties.

What I learned, however, was the value of truly finding myself, locating who I was, while yet not being "at home" in my own life, at its most intimate core. Though this was not what I had sought—as with many people, I wanted a solid marriage, a home, financial stability, etc.—I discovered the incredible power of finding a source of spiritual strength and a determinate sense of self through embracing myself despite not being "at home" in my own life. I learned to live in some ways as a permanent pilgrim and to dwell in such an identity that is no solid identity at all.

There is nothing wrong with being at home in this world, if such a thing is possible. But the pilgrim focuses on the real core of our being, how we are and remain mysteries to ourselves, lost in the complexity of our existence, not "at home" even when we are ostensibly "at home" in our own lives.

The pilgrim, above all, honors and finds ways to maintain and learn from this state of being, even if it is the last thing one actually wants to embrace.

☙

When I stepped into the mass of bodies circulating through the sanctuary of San Pietro today, I felt nothing, no awe, no reverence, no sacrality other than what I carried in there with me. My own longings redoubled on me, forcing me to reckon with my own internal landscape. I thought of how

Saint Peter's Basilica

some saints have expressed the feeling of God's absence, sometimes over long periods of years.

I steadied myself and continued walking.

⁂

For years, every time I was in Rome, I had to visit San Pietro, had to walk through its square at all hours, day and night. It was a ritual I completed with great satisfaction, just to dwell in such proximity to its magnificence. I fondly recalled all the spaces I had explored there and all the pictures I had taken there, going to mass and touring the archaeological dig, or *scavi,* underneath it.

The cupola, the bones of Saint Peter, the tombs of the popes in the crypt, Bernini's masterpieces, and the foot of Saint Peter's statue—they had been to me the clear heart of the city; everything else ran directly through it.

This perception was of course due to the fact I had been diligent in making a concerted effort to immerse myself in Catholic tradition and ritual, even if always from a certain critical distance. Coming here seemed to offer me a reduction of that distance and to signal a willingness to accept that which I couldn't fully accept with the confirmation of my reason. The material proximity of holiness overcame my doubts and welcomed me to a space within myself that spoke louder than my thoughts. I was always grateful at an unconscious level for this ability to let go and walk along a path that spoke deeply to me.

⁂

I need at times to perform an archaeology of my own story of faith, to peel back the many layers of history that characterize my life and simply observe them as if they were on display in a museum. I want to perceive the various living strata that comprise my unique narrative, embracing them all as they form a foundation. I do not wish to repress any single layer or story so that another might appear as the only, dominant "surface" account of who I am and where I have been.

I want rather to see the foundation, the earthquakes, the dynasties, the embarrassments, the attempts to bury or conceal now exposed, the borrowings from others, the leaps forward and the innovations—everything at once in its place and ineradicable from the larger tale of my life.

Here, my Protestant roots have a permanent home, as does my conversion to Catholicism, the hours spent in prayer, the teachings of Scripture on my lips, and the loss of faith that set me adrift from organized religion recognized and embraced. Here is my family's influence, the books I have read and loved, the friends I am lost in conversation with, and the desire to give a foundation to my son. Here is my marriage, its joys and despairs, here is my divorce, with much the same scales in balance. Here are my belongings and my trust. Here my questions and suspicions.

Everything fitting together in just such a way as to constitute my self.

I have long contemplated what San Pietro means to me. It is a vast expanse of architecture and art, spanning numerous centuries, as well as countless saints and popes. It is a combination of shrines and basilicas that has truly taken on a life uniquely its own. It is also the work of thousands and a home for billions of Catholics living and dead, though one pope sits at its pinnacle, and only Jesus can be said to be its true head.

Peter, as the first among peers, stands at the historical origins of the church, and his presence is everywhere, though what envelops me on this particular day is the mystery of a persistent tension between belief and unbelief that seems to descend from the massive dome at the same time as I feel myself being swept up toward it.

The apostle Peter was once locked in a tremendous tension with Paul, the latter being an upstart follower of Christ who felt that the gentiles were allotted a share at Christ's table as much as the Jews. Peter, however, maintained that one must first become a Jew in order to be a follower of Jesus, just as all of the disciples had been. This seemed to be something Jesus himself had intentionally chosen.

In the end, and after some bit of divine intervention if the biblical book of Acts is to be believed, Peter came to see Paul's point of view, and embraced non-Jews within the earliest forms of the church. The tension between Jewish tradition and identity and gentile cultures and philosophies was not to go away, however. If anything, the tension became constitutive of Catholicism itself.

☙

There is an unending contrast between the Hebrew and Greek elements of Christianity, and they are as rich in their tension as they are impossible to separate within the church. The both/and mentality of Catholicism prevents one from ever severing the connection between Peter and Paul, despite their differences, just as one cannot permanently separate the materiality of faith from its spiritual dimensions.

For me, there was also a permanent tension between belief and unbelief that seems forever in-built and determining of what faith is truly about, though it is one that we still haven't learned to acknowledge or cultivate.

☙

Though the tourism and crowds of the city often speak loudly of the secular culture that resides in permanent critique of the pilgrim's way, to walk under the dome of St. Peter's is to be reminded of the awe-inspiring nature of faith, precisely through its material embodiment. One's eyes are drawn upward at the same time that one is forced to face their own smallness—and this is how the faith comes to rest on the individual soul who submits their body to the immensity of the tradition as perceived through its edifice.

In this sense, the mystery of faith comes to resemble, or rather is made manifest, in the existing tensions that cannot be reconciled or joined without remainder.

There is a power in being reminded of one's smallness, in not being able to take the usual routes offered for avoiding this confrontation with oneself. This is also why the pilgrim must unplug from the ordinary, as Dorothy Day once put it. There is no room for cameras or phones, or any technological distractions, and it is not just because these things might disrupt one's focus.

Each time a picture is taken, we attempt to capture and subvert the moment rather than be present to it. Each attempt to reach out to one's friends and family through social media subverts the pilgrim's solitary

Sacred Pilgrim, Secular Pilgrim

journey, causing us to potentially miss the benefit of what lies waiting for us. We become blinded to those presences the pilgrimage seeks to reveal when we are busy trying to secure our relations in the world.

We become as such potentially numbed to the tensions that comprise our lives, and our faith, when we seek to streamline our communication networks so that we might stay perpetually plugged in to them. There is no chance that we enter into an encounter with otherness, even *with the other standing right before us*, when our every effort is made to avoid such encounters.

※

It is not just the art or the history that speaks to a person here. It is not just the relics or the altars that suggest another reality to us. It is not just the history that jumps out to us from nearly every corner of the church. There is something powerful to be absorbed in simply letting the unresolved tensions of the church, of belief and unbelief, wash over the body, immersed as it is in the spaciousness of the building itself.

The mystery of faith is found through allowing the materiality of life to overwhelm and overtake the spirituality of one's self, and feeling that this is how things should be, no matter how disruptive of our everyday routines such an action is.

The pilgrim is the one who not only welcomes such things; they are the one who is willing to make long and difficult journeys in order to see that they do indeed happen.

※

To say that I am perpetually caught between a fullness and an emptiness within is to say that I am caught between belief and its absence. I am at once both a religious believer and an atheist, with no need to resolve this tension, but only a desire to further cultivate an indifference that cares not how I identify myself any longer. This indifference is itself a spiritual impulse to exist beyond the desire to seek refuge in either identity, only to let go more fully—always more fully—of what I had once thought it essential to maintain as part of my identity, but which now I am all too ready to disregard. To my mind, this indifference is the indifference of the pilgrim to the physical toll the pilgrimage takes on one's mental and physical limits.

I wish only now to sit quietly in an undefined and uncertain space that more accurately reflects the patience I must hold out for both myself and the one who stands before me, whomever that may turn out to be.

It crosses my mind on numerous occasions that encountering the divine in a particular space would be much the same experience: to be humbled before an uncertain but profound presence that we cannot define in any real way, try though we might to capture its essence and communicate it to others. We will always be at a loss in such space, in such moments—and seeing my life as a pilgrimage differs little from this openness.

The loss of faith I feel acutely within me finds its reflection in the mostly empty churches I sit in, or the ones that are devoid of a spiritual sincerity, rather full to the brim with tourists.

My atheism is inextricable from my faith, from my own personal collapse and eventual rebirth, and I have no wish to hide or obscure this fact. I believe moreover that the only way to enter into the brightness of the light is to first allow the dark interior to engulf us and enrich us with its force. Not backing away from the abyss of meaning is the only way to find a meaning that cannot be destroyed so easily.

Under the Dome

He briefly describes different popes' attitudes toward Vatican II—He affirms that even in a space of political power, there are moments that seem to transcend the ordinary run of things—For him, San Pietro may be the last place one can make an emotionally meaningful pilgrimage—He believes that pilgrimage is the journey of walking through this world awakened to life in whatever space we might truly find and embrace it

As these examples illustrate, and no doubt countless others could be produced, San Pietro's expansive interior, cold marble, and austere atmosphere give the appearance of formality, enough to invoke a court of law or political amphitheater. The building itself is a performance of power that reflects the many popes and cardinals whose presences still linger in the sanctuary, and even more so in the dark corners and recesses where whispers intimate more than political bargaining.

From the perspective of the pilgrim, what kind of an atmosphere is this, that could be so wedded to ecclesial power as to almost stultify the free movement of the spirit under its dome? Is there anything to be gained from making the trek here in order to immerse oneself in a spirit that also moves beyond its dome?

ஐ

Even in such fixed spaces of political power, however, there are moments that seem to transcend the ordinary run of things.

In the center of the sanctuary floor is an inscription commemorating the beginning of the Second Vatican Council with John XXIII on October

11, 1962. Pope John XXIII was elected as an interim pope, expected not to live long, but who actually shocked the world by calling for a Second Vatican Council, which opened the Catholic Church to the modern world, effectively reversing the atmosphere of anti-modernism within the church.

Though he died before the council finished—and so it had to be completed by Pope Paul VI—he instigated revolutionary change within the Church that is still controversial and contested to this day. Indeed, many read the papacies of John Paul II and Benedict XVI as attempts to subvert Vatican II, while the papacy of Francis appears to some as a return to its ideals.

As but one reaction against this council, Archbishop Marcel Lefebvre broke off from the Catholic Church in order to found his own, more traditional and orthodox community.[1]

۞

John XXIII insisted that Vatican II, as it is also called, not have any condemnations or excommunications, but rather that it be a conciliar effort to listen to the needs of the Church.[2] It therefore brought about an openness to other religions, to laity within the Church, to vernacular masses, and so much else that allowed a new, more modern spirit to inhabit Catholicism.

Subsequently, Pope Paul VI spent most of his own pontificate trying to hold together a divided church, a task at which he mainly succeeded, despite its extreme difficulties. It was during these efforts that he expanded the college of cardinals, opening the doors to many cardinals from diverse parts of the world, and began the phenomenon of the traveling pope, which was exercised with vigor by John Paul II after him.

No matter what one thinks of the Second Vatican Council, there is no doubt that it brought about an openness to the world that has created new perceptions of faith in the modern world. Though some might see it as a capitulation to worldly forces of secularization, and others might see it as a breath of fresh air that opens the Church to much needed change, the council at least set a new precedent in that it was not called to censure or excommunicate anyone, but rather to remind the Church of what it is to itself, and so consequently for the world as well.

1. Duffy, *Saints and Sinners*, 362.
2. Duffy, *Saints and Sinners*, 358.

San Pietro, in its splendor and sterility, may seem like the last place one should make an emotionally meaningful pilgrimage. Yet such spaces can often be ideal for removing oneself from the ordinary flow of life and to engage oneself in bold and profound bouts of contemplation. The austerity and emptiness of its massive interior can serve as the spark of transcendence from the everyday.

It is incredibly shortsighted to reject idealistic desires and ivory tower spaces of thought and contemplation, as they are often the most practical—and human—things we can do in the face of the various crises we routinely face. Prayer, from a religious point of view, should be added to this list too, for it is a "waste of time" that, much like a good friendship, offers us so much through its refusal to take part in the normal economies of our world.

From a much wider perspective, to locate a presence beyond ourselves, and to let such a transcendent experience speak to us, often through our capacities for empathy and understanding, is an inherently compassionate and ethical encounter. These encounters are ground zero for human relations and we need to cultivate them further, not just relegate them to those who enjoy the intellectual life.

I recall years ago, on my first major hike up a 14,000-foot peak in Colorado one summer, how disillusioning it was to continuously think that I was just about to reach the summit of a mountain only to discover again and again that it was a mirage and that I had much farther to climb. The disillusionment was the result of my own false perceptions and it quickly dissipated upon eventually reaching the actual peak later in the day.

Pilgrimage for me is about working through the constant disillusionment of not knowing when the peak will be reached, but carrying on in the belief that it will be summited nonetheless. Encountering tourist hordes, a sudden disenchantment with a once sacred space, the loss of belief or the physical and emotional costs that such journeys take on us all exact their toll. Pilgrimage is about carrying on, and being carried by others, when we have lost the will to journey at all.

Under the Dome

※

Though my faith in religious, doctrinally based faith has eroded, my faith in the process of pilgrimage has not, an ironic twist that, admittedly in some ways, speaks to the truth embedded deep within such religious practices in the first place. My openness to pilgrimage and to making one in the heart of the most traditionally Catholic of cities does not displace my disbelief, as it does not suddenly take away my experience of disillusionment. But I no longer expect my disillusionment to disperse once and for all. I expect to make peace with its presence, learn to see life from another point of view, find healing and wholeness amidst all of life's craziness, and to keep on walking, enriched by the experience.

Maybe, some will say, this is not what a pilgrimage is about. It is rather a sincere, religious journey to the site of a miraculous appearance, to the shrine of a saint said to grant requests, to bathe in or drink from healing waters. Moreover, it must be accompanied by specific prayers or shared beliefs.

Such things may be laudable, though I harbor my doubts. But, to me, the experience of the pilgrim is far broader and more personal than any definition, limitation, or expectation we might be able to place upon it. It is the journey of walking through this world awakened to life, as it appears, in whatever space we might truly embrace it.

※

At the very moment I stood lost in thought among the colonnades just outside San Pietro I was aching to sit among a grove of aspens in a meadow like many I have visited in Colorado's wilderness areas. Nature was calling me away from history and marble, toward a sense of the sacred in another place, another pilgrimage that overlaps with contemporary notions of hiking and camping.

The "church of the wild," as Victoria Loorz has put it, was calling me from afar and I knew that, at some point, I would yield to its call just as profoundly as I had once responded to the call to come to Rome.[3]

---

3. Loorz, *Church of the Wild*.

There was a sadness in this thought, to leave behind something that had been so valuable for me for so long, but there was also a joy at having found something so meaningful to me that I couldn't wait to love it in person once again.

Contested Spaces

He presents two contested spaces: Santa Maria sopra Minerva, built over a Roman temple to Isis, and as a burial site to many popes, and the Pantheon, a pagan site and the burial site of the first king of Italy—He explains that Santa Maria sopra Minerva represents the collusion of different religious traditions and divergent views within the Catholic Church itself—The Pantheon, according to him, shows the plurality of our world today and its syncretistic desires—He points out that these contested spaces reflect the politics of personal faith today

THOSE WERE MY THOUGHTS, not only at San Pietro, as at so many other sacred spaces, but, more immediately, as I stood at the tomb of Fra Angelica in Santa Maria sopra Minerva. Fra Angelica is the patron saint of art and so too a reminder of the boldest presentation of those much-needed idealistic desires put on display before us every day.

Art, it can easily be said, serves no ostensible purpose, yet it is still essential to human life. We need the uselessness of beauty as much as we need the wastefulness of prayer and of academic conversation, in order to access profound interior parts of ourselves. This tomb, as with Rafael's or Bernini's, reminds us of the foundational role that art plays in the spiritual life.

S. Maria sopra Minerva dates from the seventh century, though the present church was actually built in the thirteenth century by the Dominican order. It was constructed on top of a temple to Isis, mistakenly thought at the time to be to Minerva, hence the church's title indicates Mary *over* Minerva, a reference perhaps to the Christianity's attempt to dominate over paganism.

The church bears Rome's only Gothic interior, despite the façade, which actually dates from 1600. Generally associated with major medieval European cathedrals, Gothic architecture—named after the Goths who invaded the Roman Empire early in Christianity's history—exemplifies the expansiveness and sovereignty of Catholic identity and is nearly absent in the buildings of Rome. Associated with French and German cathedrals in particular, Gothic style arose in the twelfth century and ended somewhere around the sixteenth, providing a bridge between Romanesque and Renaissance (Baroque) architectures.

Typically, Gothic churches and cathedrals are defined as those which include pointed arches, ribbed vaults, and flying buttresses. They are spectacularly complex in their presentation and often overwhelm the visitor with their abundant detail.

ঌ

The statue of an elephant carrying an obelisk—the shortest one in Rome—just outside Maria sopra Minerva's main entrance, was designed by Bernini. The obelisk was an Egyptian sign of the divine rays of the sun, here joined with the image of an elephant, as earth. Hence this is the symbolic union of heaven and earth, and Egyptian belief, including a belief in a resurrection of the dead, with Christian belief. Pope Alexander VII, in fact, endorsed this union of images based on the Egyptian belief in the resurrection of the dead—an original interreligious thought placed well before its time.

ঌ

There were two papal conclaves held here in the fifteenth century. The first papal conclave—the tradition of locking the cardinals in a room until they finished voting for a pope—wasn't actually held until the election of Pope Celestine IV in 1241. He lasted a short seventeen days before fleeing for his life. Another pope wasn't elected until two years later.

His short papacy was echoed by another saintly monk's election, Pope Celestine V. He became a puppet of imperial rule, only lasting six months as pope. He resigned from the papacy in 1294 in order to return to his "humble life," but was then thrown in an ecclesiastical jail cell by Pope Boniface until his death, so as to prevent schism within the Church.[1] Celestine V, however, was canonized by a later pope, Clement V, who wanted to exact revenge on Pope Boniface for imprisoning him.[2]

Pope Benedict XVI was more recently inspired by the resignation of Celestine V to submit his own resignation in 2013. He in fact visited Celestine's tomb shortly before he announced his intentions to step down. Benedict's resignation was a shock to the Catholic world and seemed to rebuff those who thought that a resignation implied an impending split or schism. It was a courageous act of letting go of power and identity, one that others leaders the world over should emulate.

ട്ട

Pope Paul IV is buried in a chapel to the right of the altar, which also contains a fresco of Thomas Aquinas presenting him to the Virgin Mary, as well as another fresco of Aquinas debating heretics and shredding their books. Paul IV, for his part, was a sixteenth-century pope who worsened relations with Protestants by strengthening the Spanish Inquisition (which even detained St. Ignatius for a time).

He also started the Roman Inquisition; suspended the Council of Trent in favor of his own dictates; formed the Jewish ghetto and made all Jews wear a yellow hat; locked up rival (liberal) cardinals in jail, accusing them of being Protestant; jailed all prostitutes; started the Index of Forbidden Books; cut off Michelangelo's pension and threatened to whitewash the Sistine Chapel, and demanded that his nude paintings and statues be covered up or repainted (something Michelangelo refused to do); appointed his nephew as a cardinal who was later removed for financial corruption; and started and supported very unpopular wars in Italy that hurt the Italian people. Paul IV also declared war on Spain, the only solidly Catholic country during the Reformation years.[3]

On the death of Paul IV, the people of Rome rioted, decapitating his statue (which had a Jewish yellow hat placed on it first). They murdered the main Roman inquisitor, ransacked the papal residence, and burned all files on the Roman Inquisition. They immediately removed his coat of arms

---

1. Duffy, *Saints and Sinners*, 159.
2. Duffy, *Saints and Sinners*, 164.
3. See Duffy, *Saints and Sinners*, 216.

from all churches, and gathered in the square outside S. Maria sopra Minerva intent on burning the church down. They were eventually talked out of this later plan by ecclesial authorities. Initially, Paul IV was quietly buried at St. Peter's, but his remains were later brought discreetly to S. Maria sopra Minerva. His papacy helped to cement Protestant hatred of the Catholic Church and his hatred of Spain alienated the ruling powers of Europe.

His successor, Pius V, was responsible for ending the Roman Inquisition and cleaning up a lot of his predecessor's messes.

※

As the Dominicans were at the forefront of the Inquisitions that swept through Europe trying to unify orthodoxy, Galileo was put on trial within the Dominican complex just behind the church. He was subject to trial under Pope Urban VIII in the seventeenth century for challenging the pope's authority, as beforehand the Church hadn't been too concerned with his ideas about the sun. It was only insofar as he challenged the order of the universe, with the pope at its pinnacle, that he fell afoul of Urban.[4]

The office of the Inquisition never actually went away but merely transformed itself into the Congregation for the Doctrine of the Faith (CDF), the Vatican branch that deals with censorships and excommunications. It has since been rebranded once again, under the pontificate of Pope Francis—now called the Dicastery for the Doctrine of the Faith—in order to spend even less time dealing with heresies and censorships.

※

Beyond the popes buried here, Saint Catherine of Siena, who was instrumental in bringing the papacy back to Rome from Avignon, rests beneath the main altar. She convinced Pope Gregory XI to leave France and return to Rome in 1377. For this, she is honored in numerous places around the city for her significant influence. She was a Dominican nun who also wrote a treatise on mystical experience that gained a wide audience. She died at the age of thirty-three, some say because she starved herself, subsisting on only the Eucharist.

---

4. Duffy, *Saints and Sinners*, 235.

Her head is preserved for veneration in Siena, Italy, her birthplace, though her body is under the main altar in Maria sopra Minerva. The room Catherine of Siena passed away in was replicated in the seventeenth century to be exactly as it was when she died. It is located just beyond the sacristy. This is the first ever transplanted interior room, or "period piece," in history—another indicator of the evolution that took place in the modern era from holy site to museum space.

※

The contested grounds of Maria sopra Minerva represents the collusion of different religious traditions, as well as divergent views within the Church itself. There is no way to purify such a space for orthodox aims, nor should there be. Its complexity speaks to the realities of existence that we would do well to grow closer to, not remove ourselves further from.

I recall, many years ago, wandering through the spectacular openness of the cemeteries of the Second World War in Normandy, France, wondering to what degree such spaces collided with the feelings of sacredness that accompanied them. To feel something sacred associated with warfare and nationalism was always a strange sensation: should this feel like holy ground? What was it that these men worshipped? What is it that anyone worships when they stand in awe upon such sites?

The list of possibilities is long and it resonates deeply with religious themes: freedom, sacrifice, determination, will, a sense of unity and camaraderie, the defense of one's values, and the elevation of courage and bravery. But are any of these things, or all of them together, enough to manifest feelings of the sacred?

These questions circulated through my mind as I sat later that day just down the street from Maria sopra Minerva, outside the Pantheon at Rome's heart, looking at the crowds gathering there, everyone waiting to step inside and have their breath taken away by a thin sliver of light falling from the ceiling onto the marble floor extending out underneath their feet.

※

Every time I enter this space, the confusion of various sacralities bats me about the head. Was this a shrine to all the gods of ancient Rome, itself a not-so-subtle tribute to the Greek pantheon of deities? Was it a Catholic church dedicated to the martyrs, Santa Maria ad Martyres—the "official" name almost no one uses to describe the place? The bones of early Christian martyrs had been carted from the catacombs and dumped *en masse* underneath the main altar in order to consecrate—some might say legitimate—an otherwise pagan shrine.

Was it perhaps also a shrine to the arts, as it contains the final resting place of Raphael, upon whose tomb is inscribed "The man here is Raphael; while he was alive, the Great Mother of All Things [Nature] feared to be outdone; and when he died, she, too, feared to die"?

Or was this place really a modern national shrine at its core?

❧

The first king of Italy, Vittorio Emmanuel II, the "Father of the Fatherland," is buried here, as is the second king, Umberto I. Vittorio Emmanuel was excommunicated from the Church at the time of his death, but was still buried here. He not only died in a state of excommunication but refused to meet with a papal envoy sent to his deathbed in order to reverse this decree. The king flatly refused this ecclesial power play, orchestrated by the Vatican in order to convince people of the pope's authority.

Vittorio Emmanuel's becoming king had signaled the end of papal power in Rome—a point that helped to form an *ultramontane* papacy in the nineteenth century as well as the Catholic Church's general rejection of modernism on the whole. It was more than a little ironic, then, that these kings of Italy who had taken so much away from papal authority are forever lying in state within a technically Catholic church.

❧

These uneasy juxtapositions raised other questions for me as well: had the Catholic Church really wrested control of the site away from its ancient Roman heritage, or had the Roman ethos won out in the end? Were all of these various manifestations of the sacred forced to co-exist for a reason, one that would never fully be sorted?

Lest we forget what Catholicism is about at its core, it might be helpful to recall that one of the great strengths of Catholicism is that it is a tradition constantly traversed by unresolved tensions. As I have already noted, its tendency to assert a "both/and" mentality has allowed it to absorb many different traditions and practices throughout the world and throughout the centuries.

Its tradition is composed of competing elements, just as its religious orders and theologians are often at odds with one another and with the Church's hierarchy. Its Scripture is a hybrid concoction of myriad elements, including Egyptian hymns and other ancient Near Eastern mythologies and literatures. The ethnic variations of the Catholic faith that incorporate local customs into their liturgies and rituals seem to be a permanent witness to a diversity that can neither be overcome nor should it ever cease.

If the tensions that comprise Catholicism were to fade away, so too would the faith itself.

It sounds paradoxical, to say the least, that someone who rightly can be called a professor of theology also professes to be an atheist. It also strikes me as more than paradoxical that the atheist that I am strives and searches for moments of transcendence in religious spaces and traditions, seeking to cultivate the spirit of the pilgrim shorn of the need to believe in specific doctrinal positions.

Like so many who wander from shrine to shrine, however, I search for epiphanies and experiences of the holy and the sacred that lift me up beyond the ordinary world and offer me a glimpse of profound poetic truths about the existence of humanity and the awe that permeates our universe seemingly without end. Most days I care little if we call such experiences of grace sacred or secular, infused with the divine presence or a reflection of our own humanity. True quests for integrity and the sublime affairs of our own hearts, I feel, need not make such distinctions.

The many complex facets of pilgrimage and its embodied reality are the perfect cipher for the complexities of the self that I carry with me as I journey toward the end. What I hold within me is a multifaceted self that I am simply incapable of describing in any singular or succinct way. Just as pilgrimage is about loss and pain, liminal states, cultivating an openness, receiving gifts, being lost in wonder and so much more, so too am I capable of letting these varied traits open me up to my own self. Raising an awareness within myself to my own complexity means allowing myself to rest before the mystery that I am and remain to myself.

My body carries all of those tensions within it and they enrich me greatly as I simply recognize their inescapable presence.

To judge my loss of faith as wrong or bad would be to reduce the complexity of myself and what I have been through, and to do myself a great disservice. I wish rather to flood my narrative with the unresolved tensions and contradictions that serve to establish me as I am.

The Christian logic of God as victim and the uplifting of the lowliest that results has achieved its conclusion in the Pantheon today, where a temple to all the gods in an ancient context is now, on the day I choose to visit it this time, housing a display about refugees from around the world.

In this contested space of multiple sacralities—Roman, Christian, Italian—the result of this hybridity is to emphasize the new divinities (á la the Romans) by focusing on the weakest among us (á la Christianity) who take the form of the refugee (á la contemporary Italy). This, if anything, is the place where the world's spirituality is headed and the Catholic Church, at least in this context, seems to be recognizing such trends.

Here, the plurality of our world and its syncretistic desires are on display, even if such a thing is not what many within the Catholic world would like to see. Our world contains so many sacred sites—religious, nationalistic, memorialized, natural, and mysterious—that at times they converge in one place and completely overwhelm those who enter their environment.[5]

It is an inevitable blending of values and traditions that brings about something unique in this specific location, in this sacred site that cannot be replicated elsewhere and, indeed, should not be.

---

5. See the catalog of sites in Westwood, *On Pilgrimage*. See also the narrative of exploring a diverse number of holy places in Shrady, *Sacred Roads*.

Tensions in the Body

He visits a small church named after Ss. Giovanni e Paulo—He is reminded of the many tensions that the Catholic Church embodies—He is drawn to these tensions and does not wish to dispel them—He finds these tensions expand his vision in multiple historical directions at once—He also finds that these irresolvable tensions serve to further heighten other pressures regarding the dimensions of sacrality in our world

As I exit the Pantheon, I notice how each day in Rome begins for me with no plan and no formal writing agenda. I simply begin walking, exploring, and letting my mind wander, and such gestures are more than enough to fuel my imagination.

Perhaps my days of sitting in front of a computer screen to "produce" a manuscript are coming to a close, or perhaps it was just the impetus I needed at this point in my life to write this particular book.

What I do know is that physical movement inspires me, prods forth a dynamic between the space I enter and observe and the thoughts and words that accompany me in and through that space. It is similar to my experience of reading Hegel while walking to and from work some years ago, as the density of his philosophical system seemed to unfold more clearly when I was in constant motion, not while seated and trying to stay awake in my chair.

My embodied life cannot be separated from my work and I would not want to detach them from each other.

I walk and I walk and I walk, seemingly without end, seemingly only to see my feet placed one in front of the other before me. I veer away from the crowds and toward lesser known spaces for reflection and the calmness it inspires.

Visiting the smaller basilicas of Rome has multiple benefits. Fewer people being the main one, but also more time to explore and to contemplate whatever one might confront that day. If a chance encounter with an epiphany is going to take place, it is most likely going to happen because one has the physical and mental space to be receptive to whatever such a thing turns out to be.

≫

It was an early morning excursion through the Metro in Rome that led to my exit near the Colosseum, a brief stroll past the gathering hordes under the Arch of Constantine and a scramble up a hill to the church of Ss. Giovanni e Paulo.

About halfway there, I stopped for a moment on a small piazza to watch the onslaught of commuters loop around the Circo Massimo, an ancient race track for chariots. I pondered the ruins, both sparse and dominant, that dot the hillside just across the street.

There was never any doubt that my route would be less crowded. I just wasn't as prepared to be so suddenly removed from the frenetic activity, as if one less careful step would immediately thrust me back into the midst of it all. It was dizzying to confront the boldness of the contrast alone.

Taking a moment to realize how I was, in the briefest sense, no longer immersed in that world was also somehow helpful, part of the journey I had undertaken by coming back to Rome, coming back to something I knew was here, but which had continuously eluded me. Every time I entered one of these storied Roman basilicas, something emerged from the stone and marble to envelop me. In that presence I felt entirely comfortable, despite my inability to name it.

≫

I was drawn to this small, ancient church in particular because it contained an archaeological excavation underneath its foundations, one that pointed

Tensions in the Body

more directly backward in time to the *domus ecclesia*, or "house church," that had once allegedly been the central gathering places of the earliest Christians. Though most of the original "house churches" in Rome are disputed, as it may have been later ecclesial tampering that provided their titles (as "tituli"), there is undoubtedly a rich history recalling such legacies behind each building.[1]

The church above these Roman houses was certainly both ancient and noteworthy—indeed it is known as *La Chiesa Dei Lampadari*, or "the church of the chandeliers"—though it lacks the visceral splendor that characterizes so many other churches scattered amidst the Roman ruins. Most times I had stumbled upon it, in fact, there was a wedding celebration festively taking place underneath its otherwise dull façade.

Coming to this place in particular, sitting quietly in its presence, or in the park just across the street, was a reminder of the many tensions that the Catholic church embodies between the *domus ecclesia* ("house churches") and the palatial splendor of Constantinian Christianity, but also of those between the horizontal life before my eyes and the vertical one that draws our attention upward, beyond ourselves.

Tensions also exist between egalitarian visions of an institutional order and the hierarchical, male-dominated structures that comprise its reality; diocesan structures and religious or monastic orders; the never-ending tension between conciliar bodies (councils of bishops) and the monarchical-papal forms that have drawn so much attention; ancient Roman religion and Christian triumphalism; and even (later) Protestant "house churches" and the problematic Catholic hierarchy that the Reformers so steadfastly critiqued and resisted.

These tensions are paralleled, and at times combined, with tensions between rich and poor Catholics and male—including an all-male hierarchy—and female Catholics. There are also tensions between "liberal" and "conservative" Catholics, typically reflecting the contrast between Vatican II supporters and its critics (or, for some, Vatican II versus Vatican I, heretical versus orthodox doctrines). These tensions are frequently portrayed as

---

1. Taylor, Rinne, and Kostof, *Rome*, 143–45.

monarchical versus democratic forms, or a (Roman) centralized Church versus a decentralized Church.

Mirroring these tensions are also the ones between papal sovereignty and conciliar decision-making structures, following Christ versus following the Spirit, as well as hierarchies versus egalitarian relations.

Raised Protestant, later having converted to Catholicism, and subsequently leaving religion behind as a matter of personal identification, I am traversed by these tensions and unable to look away from them. They are somehow constitutive of my beliefs as much as what I do not believe at the same time. There is another tension as well, one that is manifested in the very building itself in so many ways.

I am consistently baffled and awed by the presence of an ancient sacred space located underneath a contemporary one. The alignments of history beckon. I cannot say that the tension this juxtaposition introduces is ever resolved. In fact, I think it is quite the opposite: the un-resolvability is itself the main attraction.

What appears as a site for sacrality to manifest itself has a secret, has a past, a history, a series of revelations potentially always in store for us, which just may serve to subvert the sense of sacredness we accompany on the surface of things.

༄

What this insight does for me is to expand my vision in multiple historical directions at once. I am transfixed by the potential itself, utterly captivated by the limitless possibilities that history opens up before me.

I find too that this irresolvable tension only serves to further heighten other tensions within my purview regarding the dimensions of sacrality in our world: is the divine to be found in the immaterial spirit or the material nature of life? Is the experience of the divine a necessity or a contingent happening that cannot be controlled in any way? How do wealth and splendor fare against the rugged poverty of faith? Will a genuine encounter provoke strength and resolve or vulnerability and weakness? Am I fated to end up where I am or am I free to choose? Is there some law guiding all manner of things or does grace flow freely, wherever it will?

There is nothing particularly striking about the interior of Ss. Giovanni e Paulo, nothing except the fact that this entire line of questioning haunts me every time I am here, in this particular space. Nowhere else am I as haunted by these tensions as I am in this particular geographical and ecclesial space, and that makes this site one very dear to me, even if its uniqueness is imperceptible to most.

There is an undeniable inquiry that permeates my entire being when I walk up the hill toward this site, one that continues to call my entire identity into question. For this, I am unendingly filled with gratitude.

Catechesis of the Relics

He comes to Santa Croce in Gerusalemme—He distinguishes between the solitude that helps to recapture the essence of pilgrimage and modern forms of isolation—He discovers that this chapel of relics draws the pilgrim inward—For him, Santa Croce is not just a symbol of faith, but the faith itself—He respects those who come to the chapel of relics to find a union of the spiritual and the material, a union which comprises life—He also welcomes disruptions and his openness provides renewal

UNDERSTANDING HOW THE INTERRUPTION of life is key to a life lived fully is another way toward comprehending the nature of the Catholic sacramental life. Catholicism's near obsession with the materiality of faith is not an aberration. It is the fundamental structure of life itself, a point well worth underscoring in a world so often bent on abstraction from embodied reality.

To claim that supernatural elements permeate the natural world, that the invisible exists within the visible or that the divine inhabits the human, is to claim that life as we know it, as we dwell in it, is constantly haunted and potentially dissected by that which is beyond it. Rather than this being the condition of a failure to connect, however, it is the definition of the properly human. The transcendent lies within the immanent, not forever apart from it, and humanity's task has been, and will forever be, to recognize the truth of this reality.

When trying to grasp the appeal of the material objects of faith inside a Catholic church, one must start with this premise. The many saints' bones and bodies, the clothing worn by holy persons, the artifacts said to belong to Mary or Jesus or St. Francis or Padre Pio—these are all signs of a world where the human is split at the seams by something that exceeds them and that somehow also abides in the physical, natural world in which we live.

Pilgrimage is where we work out the embodied tensions and contradictions that comprise us. We need the physical space to redraw our inner world, to stretch ourselves toward an infinite horizon and to allow ourselves to reconceive of who we are and what we bear with us at all times.

It takes some effort of concentration and an intentional approach in order to locate moments of calm, silence, and an inner meditative state while wandering through the many distractions of modern travel. Sitting in airports, train stations, riding in taxis and on buses, you can easily lose a sense of what it means to be a pilgrim today.

Walking in solitude helps to recapture the essence of pilgrimage because it isolates the mind and body at a pace that can be more easily adapted to spiritual contemplation.

This form of isolation is not the same thing as modern forms of alienation that spill out into the seemingly endless expanses of loneliness and its accompanying desperations. Solitude is not alienation because it grounds and connects us to all that lies around us, to the people we love and to those strange to us as well.

As I write these words on a train from Naples to Rome, I feel the presence of those around me more acutely, a welcome sensation that leaves me filled with a genial energy. Hence, the exhaustion I feel physically on pilgrimage is not the same as other experiences of fatigue, for something deep within me—the soul—is being replenished though the body is taxed.

This crucial difference is very important to note, however, as it opens new windows into the experience of being human, of having a body and of our relation to it. We are enriched by those experiences and ideas and connections that take us beyond ourselves and place us in closer proximity to others and to the beauty of life itself, to sacred encounters and to the emptiness that frightens us all the more as we seek to avoid it.

All of this comes flooding into my mind when I stand in the small courtyard before Santa Croce in Gerusalemme. The very church was built on soil brought back in ancient wooden ships from Jerusalem just so that Helena, the mother of the Roman Emperor Constantine, might be able to worship on the holiest of soil in the world, the very ground that Jesus himself had once walked on.

Sacred Pilgrim, Secular Pilgrim

From its inception, this church would be dedicated to the materiality of faith, to a catechesis of the relics, as the church itself describes it, a utilization and passing along of the "proper" faith through its material manifestations of holiness.

🖋

Though the interior of the church today is rather less than noteworthy, it is the chapel of the relics that draws pilgrims inward. A slightly inclined slope, mimicking the hill Jesus had to climb on the way to his crucifixion, forces the pilgrim to walk upwards through the stations of the cross before standing for a moment before some of the relics that Helena had brought back from the Holy Land. Thorns said to be from Jesus' crown, pieces of the true cross upon which he was martyred, the finger of "doubting" Thomas, the nails that had pierced Jesus' body—each of these things take pride of place in a small chapel serving to remind pilgrims of how faith can only be narrated through the material that makes up our world, not in defiance of it.

It is easy to understand why pilgrims coming to the original chapel on the other side of the sanctuary were frequently seen stealing dirt from the floor until it was covered over to prevent further theft. It is the same reason that bones of the saints and martyrs were often liberated from the catacombs by the faithful: being able to hold a piece of the presence in one's hands was a salve to suffering, a reassurance in times of crisis, a reminder of what could not be seen, but also, and perhaps most significantly, it was a moment of recognizing how the materiality of life itself, that which seemed to contain no meaning in and of itself, was somehow also intimately bound up with the establishment of meaning in our world.

The unknown is simply and unmistakably part of everything that is stated.

Whatever we present to ourselves as essential to our understanding is undone by something that we will never understand. Our failure to represent the reality of the world is not what negates meaning in the world; it is the only way in which meaning can enter the world at all.

🖋

Santa Croce, or the Holy Cross, is not just a symbol of faith. It is the faith itself, just as the sacrament of the Eucharist is not just a symbol of Jesus' body but the actual body of Christ. This is a subtle but radical point to underscore: even if one does not believe in the Catholic doctrine of transubstantiation, it is the reading key needed to understand humanity. We are a mystery to ourselves in precisely the same measure.

Material reality matters to the creation of meaning to such a degree that we can say that, at some point, the symbolic dimension fails to provide an adequate account, leaving the material itself to claim credit for its articulation. Transubstantiation matters, for Catholics, but also for everyone, I would wager, because it describes the limits of human understanding. That is, there must be a point at which meaning continues after the symbolic has ceased to bear all the possible meaning in our world.

Material reality itself, at such points, is oversaturated with meaning and so continues to speak to us well beyond the words and symbols that we use to communicate with one another.

I do not know what Martin Luther felt as he climbed up the Scala Santa, if he ever did. But I know that he was dismissive of the materiality of human existence, so much so as to prompt him to latch onto the symbolic dimension alone. Yet to deny the intricate intimacies of our material existence and embodiment is to miss a crucial piece of the fabric of humanity itself.

I have no doubt that mustering a critique and eventual rejection of the Catholic Church's ills with regard to material possessions and status would take a great deal of courage and confidence, and would require much correcting of political rhetoric. But, in the end, I think that Luther overshot the mark in moving humanity one step further away from comprehending its connection to the sublime entrance of what cannot be symbolized but only embraced, in the materiality of flesh. Though this suggestion will risk the possibility of turning every sacrament into a potential fetish-object, it also contains the possibility of transforming every fetish into a sacrament.

Our relationship to the conditions of our own material existence is complicated, to be sure, but it is not something we can do without altogether either. At Santa Croce, as at Sainte Chapelle in Paris, where relics are given a prominent place, I feel the relevance of these thoughts moving me beyond what I can see, not toward some deity in the heavens, but toward that which I can never fathom and which I should never wish to.

※

I am reminded of my desire never to learn the names and configurations of the many constellations in the night sky, never to master the names of the trees and flowers that dot the beautiful landscapes that I love being immersed in, never to know the names of the fish that I catch in the rivers I wade in, for these are things I love deeply and so must respect the mystery of, even if just in part, even if by remaining foolishly naïve about them to some degree, all done with an unending acknowledgment of my limitations.

I am struck too, every time I see it, by the ancient statue of the Roman goddess Juno that stands unidentified on the way to the subterranean chapel in Santa Croce, for a large wooden cross has been placed in her arms as if it naturally belonged there. Like the Egyptian columns that support many of the churches in Rome, the Catholic Church has placed foreign objects at its base as if they justified Christianity's claims about itself. This tactic differs little from the Judaism at Christianity's own foundations and the many ancient near Eastern religious traditions that lie at the base of Judaic Scripture and tradition. The mystics and lack of full understanding spread deep into our roots and overtake us.

※

I have the utmost respect for those who come here to find a union of the spiritual and the material that comprise one's life. Even if many such relics are dubious in origin—and the shroud of Turin ranks high on this scale (a replica is on display here)—there is something very human about recognizing the sacramental (mysterious) nature of how spirit joins flesh, as well as the fascinating gap between them.

Religion often—powerfully, wonderfully—provides a way for people to suture these seemingly separated, and yet inseparable, realms; to provide an integrity and coherence to one's understanding of themselves. If the veneration of a particular holy object allows one to feel more at home in their own body, then so be it, and may such practices not cease anytime soon.

I enter the church in silence, interrupting even the words that normally run through my mind, interrupting the flows and patterns that characterize my habits and routines, of thought, of movement, of everything that constitutes my daily life. Because I welcome such disruptions and because it is my openness to them that provides a renewal I have been longing for, I allow other disruptions to enter the moment as well.

For example, I take no pictures, I talk to no one, I close my eyes, I allow only sound—and its absence—to speak to me. I feel the space around me, as it rests on the periphery of my bodily sense of sitting down in a cold chair before this altar, under this high vaulted ceiling painted a deep blue among a variety of stars. When I eventually open my eyes, I let the art and its colors restore their meaning to me, but this time, unlike when I first entered the church's doors, as if for the first time, as if I had never seen them before, as if they were trying desperately to say something to me, just me.

I do not know if this attentiveness to the moment as it rises to meet me, as I welcome its presence, is what might be considered as an experience of transcendence, but it feels so to me and I allow it to wash over me, purify me of the habitual routines that often inadvertently produce a blindness to the world around me.

I do not know what the eagle or mountain lion feel when they face the sunrise each morning within the forests and mountain tops they inhabit, but I imagine something possibly as pure as this moment as it unfolds before me.

Consumerism

He reflects upon the major retail center on Via del Corso, running straight from the Piazza del Popolo, where Goethe once lived—He compares his objections against the invasion of capitalism to Luther's protestations against the corruptions that plagued Rome in the sixteenth century—For him, this consumerism within Rome gives rise to reflections on pilgrimage and a desire to commune with the past

The contrast between such moments and the average day of walking through more crowded sections of Rome is stark, and needs to be addressed.

On the Via del Corso, running straight out from the Piazza del Popolo, there is a plaque designating the fact that, at one point in time, the German writer Goethe lived there. This unique cultural heritage seems somewhat dulled by the fact that the main source of attraction to the building right now is a discount jewelry store and another selling high quality, expensive soaps and so-called "bath bombs."

Rome's current tourist aura stems from locales such as these where the overlap between history and consumerism is rife. I wonder too if the existence of such tensions lessens the experience of being in the city and what, if anything, can be done about it.

There are some voices today who feel that modern humanity no longer experiences reality as directly as it once did, that everything is now buffered, with a critical, perhaps even skeptical, gap existing between every experience and the person who does the experiencing.

Rome, for the most part, is a premodern relic cast out into a modern world where authentic experience—whatever such a thing is or is not—seems distant at times, especially where the clear experience of so many people visiting the city seems to be either about taking selfies, shopping, or sampling local cuisine. These activities seem only to underscore the distance which most people keep with regard to whatever core lies deep within the history of the city.

&

I suppose my objections against the ever-encroaching influence of consumerism into Rome are probably no different than Luther's protestations against the corruptions that plagued the city when he journeyed here as a pilgrim in the early sixteenth century. This time, however, it is not the Church who peddles its fetishes (relics and indulgences) but capitalism and its many commodities.

It is easy to stand at a critical distance from such economies and condemn them for invading what could otherwise exist as a purer spiritual journey, but the truth is that a moderation of desire with relation to consumerism would prove a most helpful remedy.

To not get caught up in the cult of shopping and to simply purchase things based on need can counter capitalism's sweeping influence, should we choose to limit ourselves. Such individual responses cannot always directly address the tragedies of environmental degradation or global poverty, but they are a step in the right direction in terms of personal responsibility and the eventual lessening of those catastrophes that linger daily over our heads.

&

For its part, the Reformation's main impulse was to return to an "original" church (pre-Constantinian) that never quite existed as the Reformer's might have imagined it. Mussolini, much later, desired to return to a Roman imperialism that would never have matched his image of it. Both Mussolini and the Catholic Church of the late nineteenth and early twentieth centuries dug deep into the earth under Rome for a glimpse of a past that can never actually be resurrected.

Sacred Pilgrim, Secular Pilgrim

All we have is the present moment, though so many of us long to touch Peter's bones, to lower a handkerchief into Paul's tomb, to touch the hem of Christ's cloak, and to kiss the Jubilee door as we enter a major cathedral.[1]

I too feel what perhaps every pilgrim feels as they long for such presences. I too seek the quiet and to be at a remove on sacred ground looking for an encounter. I too feel the physical toll upon my body as I walk mile after mile throughout the city's many back routes to its favored locations.

I do not hope for supernatural interventions, and I do not believe the weight upon me will be miraculously lifted by divine fiat.

But I do believe it will appear this way someday, in hindsight, after I locate the life that brings me a joy I currently do not know.

※

Fate will be the retrospective framing through which I reread my present, satisfied that everything, or the important things at least, have found their proper order. Love, in fact, is the experience of being handed back in proper order the things of your life that you have given over to the beloved.

And if I never reach such a place, if I never settle into such a rhythm, life will remain a tragedy for me, as it has for so many others. Such is the sheer contingency and precarity of existence, and yet I know of no other one to which I might cling.

---

1. See Eleanor Clark's rich description of a Jubilee Year pilgrimage environment in Rome in her *Rome and a Villa*, 211–35.

A Pilgrim's Church

He focuses on the basilica of Santa Maria Maggiore—He presents a convergence of many aspects of church history—Colonization, papal authority, pilgrimage, and the history of Marian devotion all appear on this sacred site—How learning to be a pilgrim means learning to construct an internal order that gently shelters—Building a chamber of solitude, not to reject the world but to find stability and solace in its midst

TRYING TO AVOID THE contingency of existence, the Church often compromised its mission by aligning itself with power and privilege, violence and oppression. The power and sovereign displays of imperial Rome, the looting of foreign lands and the assertions of dominance, all trickled slowly into the Catholic Church's sense of its own prominence, in Rome and far beyond.

I cannot help but reflect on this transition of imperial power when I step into the Spanish-controlled major basilica of Santa Maria Maggiore, where the exploitation of the "New World" led to the splendor of this sacred dwelling.

Of all the churches of Rome, this one most closely resembles, for me at least, the atmosphere of a medieval pilgrim church, with the devout combing every side chapel, confessional, and altar for a solitary moment of spiritual insight. I have witnessed groups of pilgrims celebrating mass together, silent pilgrims in adoration before the exposed eucharistic body, and innumerable persons gathered before an icon of Mary said, probably inaccurately but significantly nonetheless, to be written by the hand of the Evangelist Luke.

Sacred Pilgrim, Secular Pilgrim

It is to the ceiling that my eye is most often drawn, however, as the solid veins of gold that line the wooden frame along with the bright hues of red and blue were said legendarily to originate in the Americas, brought back by Spanish conquistadors to honor their king and queen, as well as the Queen of Heaven.

It is perhaps fitting, though ironic, that many of the countries looted by their Catholic conquerors are themselves devoted to the Virgin Mary, often claiming her presence among them as evidence of her protective guidance of their lands and peoples. Her attentiveness to the poor in particular strikes a vibrant contrast with the wealth on display here in Rome, where a fair amount of the treasures of the Americas eventually made their way.

The gilded ceiling was made possible, at least according to legend, with gold brought back by Columbus, or possibly those conquering the Incan empire, and given to Ferdinand and Isabella of Spain who, in turn, gave it to Pope Alexander VI, another Spaniard. The church has sometimes been called "the golden basilica" for this reason, and it is still technically under the patronage of Spain.

Restoration work now has many questioning if there is real gold in the ceiling or if it was previously removed. The history of the ceiling in this church, however, calls to mind the colonial activity of the Church at this time in history, harkening back to the decision of Pope Alexander VI in 1493 to divide the new world into two regions, one for the Spanish and one for the Portuguese.[1] Catholic missionary efforts were heavily pronounced within these new territories, though the rights of the Indigenous peoples were often not respected.[2] Part of this happened because, at this time in history, popes did not appoint local bishops, but left this to each nation, which chose bishops according to their interests.[3]

༄

Despite colonization and enslavement, 175 million of 350 million Christians in Africa were Catholic in 2000.[4] Perhaps some of this is due to the fact that Christianity espouses a message of hope and liberation that has

---

1. Duffy, *Saints and Sinners*, 228.
2. O'Collins and Farrugia, *Catholicism*, 81.
3. O'Collins and Farrugia, *Catholicism*, 82.
4. O'Collins and Farrugia, *Catholicism*, 84.

spoken to oppressed peoples for centuries, as with slaves in the United States, for example.

The Jesuits were often very good at enculturation, or taking on aspects of Indigenous traditions and peoples whom they lived among, especially in the East. This led, at times, to problems with the Catholic hierarchy, as the Jesuits appeared at times to concede too much of their Catholic identity to distinctly different cultures, dressing like Confucian sages, for example, during the Chinese Rites Controversy in the seventeenth and eighteenth centuries.

It has also been difficult historically to disentangle European cultural and political interests from religious or missionary ones (e.g., St. Francis Xavier's translated question to those being baptized in India in the sixteenth century was "do you wish to join the caste of the Europeans?," not "do you want to be followers of Christ?"). Preventing Catholic missionaries from entering a country, as was the case frequently in Japan, was a way of repelling foreign political and economic influence, something the Church has never been able to fully distance itself from (see, e.g., Shūsaku Endō's novel *Silence* about Jesuit missionaries to Japan).

෴

How the Church today is able to maintain such buildings, built on the backs of injustices and the enslavement of Indigenous peoples, is a hard question to ask. There is no simple solution to this lingering problem, though following the lead of the "apologizing pope," John Paul II, in asking forgiveness for many of the Church's errors over the centuries is a beginning.

The juxtaposition of these facts, the wealth and poverty, the powerful and the voiceless, is almost too much to bear. The tensions seem symbolically portrayed by the almost nondescript tomb of Gian Lorenzo Bernini, the brilliant architect of papal Rome, which lies beneath a single step near the main altar here—a call for humility made in the midst of pride. He was the great Baroque artist who was seen too as the "megaphone" of papal orthodoxy and of the Counter-Reformation.[5]

෴

---

5. Hughes, *Rome*, 277.

This history of complicity with the horrific is slightly offset by the Church's other efforts throughout the centuries to undo some of these very same burdens. The church of Holy Trinita' degli Spagnoli in Rome was built and dedicated, in fact, to the eradication of slavery throughout the world. Altarpieces here clearly depict God's mercy being mediated through those saints who sought to eliminate the corrupt and dehumanizing practice from our world.

Though its presence does not make up or atone for the criminal acts that gave rise to many of Rome's more splendid basilicas, this church haunts the others and serves as a reminder that Catholicism's complexity is far from fully revealed to the casual observer of selected parts of its story.

✍

The Basilica of Santa Maria Maggiore was built in the fifth century, and added on to several times. Bernini, Maderno, and Michelangelo have all worked on this church in particular. In general, being called a Basilica means it has a special status conferred on it by a pope. A cathedral is the main church in a diocese, with a bishop attached to it. So, some cathedrals are also basilicas and some basilicas are also cathedrals. It is, however, the minor basilica among the four major basilicas, which include S. Pietro, S. Giovanni in Laterano, S. Paulo fuori le mura, and S. Maria Maggiore.

According to legend, the Virgin appeared to either Pope Liberius and/or a Roman patrician named John and his wife in the summer of 358 and told them to build a church where they found snow the next day (which happened to be a typically warm August 5, though historians mostly speculate that it was probably a hail storm and not snow). Nonetheless the church is known as "Our Lady of the Snows" and is the oldest Marian church in existence.

Each year white flower petals are dropped from the rooftop during vespers to commemorate this snowfall and the vision. Additionally, John and his wife are allegedly buried here under the large granite circle in the central aisle, though this may be more fanciful desiring on the part of some. Others have claimed that the present church was built on the site of a Roman temple dedicated to Juno Lucina, the goddess of childbirth or pregnant women. This conceptualization was subsequently preserved and transferred from Juno to Mary, who bore God. This is, however, a disputed legend, as it is perhaps more probable that Romans may have simply wanted to link Juno to Mary in some fashion.

Built mostly by Pope Sixtus III (432–440), who was pope during the Council of Ephesus that declared Mary the Mother of God (*Theotokos*), this church is obviously overwhelmed with Marian imagery. In some sense the unity that was brought about through the establishment of this doctrine of Mary as the Mother of God was utilized to combat the heresies of Nestorianism and Pelagianism.

According to Scripture, Mary, the mother of Jesus, was visited by an angel who announced to her that she would give birth miraculously to a son conceived through the Holy Spirit (a scene known as the annunciation). She accepted this news with rejoicing, singing a song of praise to God (termed the Magnificat). Though a somewhat minor character in the Gospels, she is nonetheless present at key moments in Jesus' life, including early prophecies about his life that cause her pain (e.g., the knife to the heart imagery), the provocation of his first miracle at the wedding at Cana when she asks Jesus to do something, and at his death on the cross.

Subsequent traditions have developed in the Catholic Church emphasizing her as the Queen of Heaven, her sinless birth (the immaculate conception), the Mother of God (*Theotokos*), the Blessed Virgin or "Ever virgin" (stressing her purity), and discussing her own ascension into heaven upon her death (the Assumption of Mary). Her subsequent appearances in specific geographical locations throughout history (Marian apparitions) have also sparked significant interest in her throughout the world, including at Lourdes, Guadalupe, Fátima, and many others. Most Protestant traditions, not having a reliance upon tradition for their doctrines, accordingly downplay her significance in the life of the church, dispensing with most of these titles and claiming (with scriptural justification) that Mary in fact had more children after Jesus' birth.

᪽

Beneath the main altar is the "most sacred part" of a pilgrim's visit to the church: the *confessio* and Altar of the Sacred Crib of Jesus, which he was supposedly placed in after his birth. This relic is adorned in crystal, silver, and gold in order to indicate the level of its importance. The crib used to be even more ornate with gold and jewels, but the church was looted in 1527 during the sack of Rome by Emperor Charles V.

The crib arrived here in the sixth century with no records and so has no historical confirmation as the "real crib." Symbolically, since Sante Croce is "in" Jerusalem (in Rome at least), Maria Maggiore is portrayed as being "in" Bethlehem, the site of Jesus' birth. This is the reason that the pope has historically held Christmas mass at this church in particular among Roman churches.

Re-created scenes of the birth of Jesus, also called nativity scenes, are ones that bring to life the birth narratives of the Gospels (and which are only presented in the Gospels of Matthew and Luke). Popularized by Saint Francis of Assisi after his trip to the birthplace of Jesus in the Holy Land, nativity scenes are now frequently associated with the Christmas season. A wide variety are possible to see, though most focus on the traditional figures of the Holy Family—Mary, Joseph, and Jesus—the shepherds, the Magi or "wise men" who were probably more akin to astrologers, the angels or angelic choir, and the various animals that would have been in the stable.

❦

The Sistine Chapel in Maria Maggiore is where Popes Sixtus IV and Sixtus V are buried. Sixtus IV was also the originator of the Sistine Chapel located today at the Vatican Museums near San Pietro, where papal elections are held.

The symbolism of the art in this smaller, less ornate chapel is a direct reference to papal power.[6] Sixtus had no problems with political intrigue, and even ordered the murder of rival Medici family members at a mass in the Duomo in Florence at one point. Pope Sixtus V was a somewhat authoritarian pope who put criminals' heads on pikes on the roads leading to the Vatican, killed priests who broke their vows of chastity, and even tried to make adultery a capital offense. He also completed the dome on the new St. Peter's, moved the obelisk from Nero's circus to in front of St. Peter's, and placed Christian imagery on many Roman monuments and columns.[7]

It was during this time of Renaissance art that the Church's theology shifted from a complete rejection of all previous "pagan" art, culture, and philosophy, to seeing Christianity as the greatest fulfillment of what had been good in such "pagan" culture. This was, of course, the time when

6. Duffy, *Saints and Sinners*, 185.
7. Duffy, *Saints and Sinners*, 189, 219, 220.

Christian humanism first began to arise.[8] Catholic thinkers, such as the great Erasmus, saw forms of secular culture arising within the Church through such initiatives.

To the left of the main altar is the Borghese Chapel, with an icon of Mary said to be painted by St. Luke, which she was said to have posed for herself. It is actually a twelfth-century (or perhaps eighth-century) painting. There is one in Constantinople, however, that also claims to be painted by Luke. This icon is called the *Salus Populi Romani*, or "salvation of the Roman people," and is seen as a sort of protector of Rome. Pope Gregory XVI in fact had it carried through Rome in 593 to avert an epidemic.

As I enter the main doors of Santa Maria Maggiore, it is hard to know what I am looking for. Even as I walk down the street toward the church, I do not know exactly what plagues me or from where my uncertainty derives. I take solace in the fact that the pilgrim doesn't have to decide between the material and the spiritual, but rests firmly on both. The sacraments, as Catholicism has long taught, are the embodiment of this refusal to separate the physical and the eternal.

I take whatever I am, in whatever state I am, into this space, aware that I might not sort any of this out, now as in the future.

☙

Pilgrims process through the *confessio* beneath the altar, itself beneath the gilded ceiling. The Sistine Chapel is to the right—though not the more famous one that resides in the Vatican museums—and a famous icon of Mary rests in a chapel to the left. But my gaze is drawn to the patterns on the floor that no one else seems much to notice.

The care with which they have been placed and the way they are overlooked speaks to me of Mary the mother, careful and caring, often unseen, yet always present in some way. A series of mosaics reflect the childhood of Jesus and the life of Mary, including some Eastern iconographic traditions about Joseph's doubting the story of her pregnancy by the Holy Spirit and her falling asleep or dying, rather than ascending into heaven as the Church later taught. The former is of particular interest in that it has been all too uncommon for the Church to endorse anything resembling doubt over the years.

---

8. Duffy, *Saints and Sinners*, 187.

Sacred Pilgrim, Secular Pilgrim

Despite its clear hagiography, I wish I could be as attentive as Mary is often portrayed to be, could allow my own child such freedom. And it is not just as a parent that she is a role model. Mary has always struck me as an isolated, solitary individual, bearing a specific pain in her heart all by herself.

The solitude of the pilgrim finds itself embodied in her journey, in her life, despite the centuries of idealizations and purity norms forced upon her. Shorn of such things, she still has the power to command attention and adoration for the significant role she plays in the larger narrative of this faith.

༄

Today there are many tourists at Maria Maggiore, snapping pictures and moving quickly from one photo opportunity to the next. It takes great effort to make space for intentional reflection within such a space, but an empty side chapel set aside for adoration provides just such a forum.

I know how hard it is to set aside time during a busy day to reflect on one's life. I more often than not force myself to take such practices seriously by shaping my vocation toward such ends, as the present writing attests. But I am only slowly and lately learning to listen to these moments when nothing comes forth, when fatigue has taken over and when I need only to let go of my thoughts rather than try to harvest those thoughts that are not forthcoming.

To be patient with myself and let nothing happen at all is the mantra I recite to myself more than occasionally these days.

༄

During the months immediately following my divorce, I could not read anything besides fiction, a genre I had kept at a distance for far too long while pursuing other, more philosophical tomes. Literature was the only refuge I could find during such internal turmoil. The novels of Haruki Murakami in particular, with their lost characters wandering in and out of mysterious circumstances, was the perfect tonic for what ailed me.

I wish I could say that I was now more "found" than I was then, but I'm still wandering, learning to embrace the lack of grounding or home that I feel while moving aimlessly through this life. I am becoming more comfortable with the general uncomfortability that permeates my daily emotional landscape.

This, I have to believe, is a sign of growth, hopefully also of some maturity.

I look out from a fifth-floor balcony onto the streets of Rome. The traffic flows without stopping, as the scooters swirl around the cars and trucks. There is such a haste and noise to it all that it is easy to project my own confusions and impatience upon the scene below, or, reciprocally, to allow the chaos below to merge with my own instabilities and uncertainties, overcoming me in the process.

Learning to be a pilgrim means learning to set boundaries where they are needed, to allow the world to be immersed in chaos while I construct an internal order that gently shelters me. To build this chamber of solitude is not to reject the world and its many wonderful and inspiring elements. It is rather to locate a stability and solace in its midst. It is to learn to love the world as a parent who loves their child, knowing their proper place always with and yet always apart from them.

The cares of the world do not disappear, they are not rejected. They are merely seen from a proper perspective. I hear the traffic from the interiority of my room, but it does not overcome me. I sit in a silence far greater than the noise. And the noise cannot overcome it.

Coda

THE PANDEMIC THAT BEGAN in 2020 put an end to a good deal of the usual routines and habits that occupied my life. Normal life, whatever such a thing was or was not, was suspended, offering unique moments of insight about what really matters most in one's life—or, in turn, presenting a dreaded absence of meaning.

The task of recognizing and respecting the self in a particular space became a heightened challenge for most of us as we looked for comfort and consolation during ambiguous and uncertain times. The ways people responded to pandemic life often said a lot about how they relate to themselves and their lives, as the suspension of typical guiding norms for daily life might be a source of despair, just as it might also enable profound reinterpretations of the layers of one's own life and history.

So much time alone for self-reflection gave rise to innumerable fantasies to live life differently, according to ideals that had not had room to surface beforehand. Something like salvation began to appear for many who could suddenly imagine life differently than it had been lived. The idea of salvation being a geographical, material reality took new form as people moved closer to loved ones or to their more ideal life.

The longing to re-enchant one's life through material conditions and one's surroundings took on new dimensions altogether.

We all have a path to walk in this life that no one else can walk. We are called, as Saint Ignatius once put it so well, not to emulate another's admirable, even saintly, life, but to live our own lives, with our own gifts and talents, to the best of our abilities.

For Ignatius, a man so wedded to the journey he had to make that he often referred to himself as "the pilgrim," discovering his vocation as the path he, and only he, had to walk down, was the preeminent model for what a pilgrim should be. And it was something that transcended any romanticized vision of pilgrimage, whether to Rome, Jerusalem, Lourdes, or Santiago de Compostela.

For Ignatius, as for so many, being a pilgrim meant following in the footsteps of Jesus. Though this is not the target at which I am aiming, what doing so meant for Ignatius is remarkably similar to my own goal: to locate an inward sacredness through a journey of discernment and transformation; to submit to the metamorphosis of my own soul in the presence of an overwhelming, greater goodness and strangeness that I cannot ignore.

Though many would argue that the point of a pilgrimage is to encounter the sacred that is uniquely present within a particular place—and which I have no qualms with and do not wish to dispute or dispel the enchanted nature of—I recognize too that a sense of sacredness flows from particular places because of the transformations that have taken place there, regardless of what the site does or does not contain today.

What of the transcendent experience of grace at the end of the pilgrimage? What of the animistic waters of Lourdes, or the sacred relic to be kissed within the large cathedral? Is pilgrimage just an inward journey of personal development or does a particular grace descend on the pilgrim because of a specific site or object said to especially house divine power?

The waters of Lourdes are sacred, I would argue, because of the prayers, hopes, desires, and healings that have happened there, no matter if they are visible or not, no matter if they are psychosomatic or not. Life is re-enchanted through pilgrimage because we are open to its possibility, not trying to control it, not trying to fabricate grace, but aware of its presence when it appears, however it appears.

It was in this sense, I believe, that the Catholic Church called itself a "pilgrim church" during the Second Vatican Council in the middle of the last century.

Built in the seventeenth century, the church of Sant'Ignazio in Rome was originally the chapel of the Collegio Romano (now the Pontifical Gregorian University, located elsewhere). Its construction demonstrated the initiatives of the Jesuit order soon after its founding members, including Ignatius himself, had died.

Its Baroque style includes the façade and an ornate, even ostentatious, theatrical décor. Yet, at the same time, it contains a pure simplicity of design with no lavish side aisles, allowing for an ease of viewing and clear lines of sight. This layout catches one's attention immediately and hides nothing.

The ceiling famously includes a trompe l'oeil "dome", meaning that there is no actual dome present in the structure, but only a perspective trick of the artist that resembles a three-dimensional object.

Sant'Ignazio, as with the other large Jesuit church in Rome, Il Gesù, has a large courtyard in front of it, which enabled early Jesuits to stage plays, preach sermons, and teach the basics of faith to crowds that gathered just outside the church doors.

I am stunned by the bustling crowd in Sant'Ignazio this Saturday morning in May. There are so many people gathered that it is hard to say what the majority are actually doing here.

I note a host of students from an American Jesuit university, other visitors lighting candles and kneeling in prayer, a queue formed to take pictures in the mirror reflecting the huge mural on the ceiling, as well as a substantial throng milling about in the nave and side chapels.

It is an impressive collection of diverse persons that speaks highly to the Jesuit sensibility for reaching out to the masses. Even the newly commissioned religious artworks seem to draw the eyes and bring a refreshing modern ethos to bear on this church's visual legacy.

My mind couldn't settle on one particular answer: are these mostly tourists or pilgrims, the faithful or those indifferent to religion altogether? Why even make a distinction between them, as I no longer cared to make such a distinction within myself?

The crowd kept pouring in and continued to marvel over this heavily occupied space before it.

I allowed myself to be carried away by each soul that entered, no longer wishing to be a solitary pilgrim, but happy to be lost in the crowd of those who gathered here with me this particular morning in the eternal city of Rome.

I doubt I will ever be able to separate the crowd into one particular group, just as I cannot clearly divide all the varied parts of myself, only learn to be more open to it all as I find and make peace with whatever I encounter.

Being in community and being married both dictate a sense of belonging. You don't have to (metaphysically) justify your existence when you benefit from being part of those identities. But, being single, you have to justify your existence every day, to yourself as much as to others. This is where you live in a state of crisis and of emergency and perhaps never feel fully at ease socially with your own life.

I realized this practical truth one night long ago when talking with two Brazilian students in Campinas, just outside of São Paulo, Brazil, who were afraid to leave their churches, despite the conservative oppressiveness with which they were too familiar, because they would then be acutely aware of having to justify their lives as they are lived now "in the darkness," on the margins of their recognized worlds, excluded and cast out from the lives they had known.

I know what it means to stay bound to what had once appeared as holy so that you don't have to feel yourself drifting further into the darkness on the edges of your world. Far too many privileged people have felt this tension rise up in them only to ignore it and to commit themselves further to an oppressive society that they do not know how to live without.

I imagine the pilgrim as the one who is willing to gather their courage and willingly begin the walk outside of a sacred community, the comforts of one's holy home, in order to wander toward another sense of holiness altogether, one wholly foreign and unknown to them.

I pray to no god, but I also do so fervently, with everything I have, that I might find such courage within myself, to leave the known and to wander seemingly without end in the unknown, asking for something sacred to appear and guide me further along the path before me.

Looking back on my pilgrimage to, and in, Rome, I sometimes want to believe that there is only one way, and so too only one history or fate, that will define my outlook on the world. I want to believe that the world can be routed through the space contained in one place, sacred to me, perhaps one city even. I want to believe that I was destined to find my fate in Rome, in one religion encountered there, and that God speaks uniquely to humanity there, in that particular place.

As Anthony Doerr has put it, "The oculus of the Pantheon, the dome of St. Peter's, the tufted pillars of the umbrella pines, and the keyhole in the green door outside the gardens of the priory of the Knights of Malta on the

Coda

Aventine Hill—they are all eyes of God. We look through them; they look through us. Everything is designed around the light."[1]

I want to believe these things because it is entirely human to do so, to search for the fulfillment of one's destiny in the presence of something larger than ourselves. To experience this sight, in the light of Rome, would unify so many of the identities that I have relied upon for so long.

But the reality is that there are other cities and other stories, (my own and those belonging to other people), which make up the innumerable possibilities for my own life. I become dizzy in this freedom, at times succumbing to its vertigo, and so I resist it and try to channel everything into one place once again so that meaning and purpose spring up from the soil that I have taken the time to cultivate.

There is nothing inherently wrong with this inevitable choice. But, to let myself experience what it means to be the uprooted pilgrim, I cannot pretend this is the only way if I want to confront and learn from my reality, to find an inner reservoir of peace and grace that might abide with me as I enter the mysterious paths that the pilgrim takes.

The freedom that lies before me is limitless and, for this reason, daunting, terrifying even, because of its infinite reach. I would like to maintain the edifice of these powers, historical and very real, that emanate from Rome, from Western civilization, the classics of its literature and the peoples who benefit still from their hegemonic hold on our world, but I have also heard the narrator from the Caribbean in Derek Walcott's epic poem *Omeros*, wandering the streets of London and failing to see anything of themselves or their people in the statues of those conquerors that line the opulent boulevards of a once mighty empire.

Rome holds its appeal as a memorial to what once was, its grandeur and its horror in equal measure. But its hold on our collective psyche will lessen—has already lessened—and its art will now sit even farther removed from the center of a much vaster global society.

Rome will however always be special to me, as parochial as this may sound, because it speaks to my own heritage, as well as its welcomed decline within my own life. My place along its streets, in its cafes, and beneath its monuments will guide me still to some degree, but I am also happy to

---

1. Doerr, *Four Seasons in Rome*, 200.

leave Rome and to look elsewhere for the spark of humanity that kindles a larger fire within me—something I have yet to more fully experience.

Faith, to me, is about the complexity of relationships, both those we maintain in community with others and those we cultivate with ourselves. Just as others will, and should, remain a mystery to us due to their complex and beautiful natures, so too will we remain unexplainable and incomprehensible to ourselves.

Faith is a set of practices and beliefs that help us to cope with and honor such complex and nuanced relations, offering us ways to deal with our guilt, shame, wrongful actions, joys, uncertainties, anxieties, hopes, betrayals, resentments, cares, loves, and so much more. Religion is a tradition honed throughout the centuries to bring some semblance of order to those varied and always mysterious relations between each of those human experiences and so many more.

For this reason alone, I have a tremendous respect for religious practices and traditions of various peoples throughout the world.

To ask if a particular religious belief is "true"—Was Jesus really God? Are there really angels? Can miracles really happen?—is a truly modern point of view, and one that frequently misses the complex nature of these embodied relationships that faith speaks to. I find such questions wonderful to ask, and to seek answers to, but also a bit of a red herring that potentially distracts us from the core of what religious faith is really about.

For a good many religious persons, to believe means to let go of their suspicion and distrust in order to let the stories and practices developed over centuries because they "worked" for so many grab hold of them and guide them. They learn to become better humans and to respect that which lies beyond them—whether a deity, another person, or themselves—by embracing a set of relations so subtle and complex that there is no way to exhaustively describe them. Words fail us at such points and symbols, songs, art, and poetry take over as the primary means of expression. And we are generally better off for simply going along for the ride.

Pilgrimage speaks to this complexity of relations by reminding us of the importance, and mystery, of our bodies and of the importance of physical space in coming to terms with that which we cannot fully express in words. Pilgrimage makes a literal space available for such nuance. It tries in so many ways to elevate that complexity to the center of our lives in order to remind us of what we carry with us each day.

Coda

I am learning about what I carry and what I have let go of, as well as what I need to pick up and cherish that much more.

Bibliography

Addis, Ferdinand. *The Eternal City: A History of Rome*. New York: Pegasus, 2018.
Adorno, Theodor W. *Aesthetic Theory*. Translated by Robert Hullot-Kentor. Minneapolis: University of Minnesota Press, 1997.
Agamben, Giorgio. *Profanations*. Translated by Jeff Fort. New York: Zone, 2015.
Augustine. *Confessions*. Translated by Henry Chadwick. Oxford: Oxford University Press, 1991.
Bissell, Tom. *Apostle: Travels Among the Tombs of the Twelve*. New York: Vintage, 2016.
Brouillette, André. *The Pilgrim Paradigm: Faith in Motion*. New York: Paulist, 2021.
Clark, Eleanor. *Rome and a Villa*. New York: Harper, 1974.
Coleman, Simon. *Powers of Pilgrimage: Religion in a World of Movement*. New York: New York University Press, 2021.
Dickens, Charles. *Pictures from Italy*. Edited by Kate Flint. London: Penguin, 1846.
Dickinson, Colby. *The Fetish of Theology: The Challenge of the Fetish-Object to Modernity*. London: Palgrave Macmillan, 2020.
———. *Theology as Autobiography: The Centrality of Confession, Relationship, and Prayer to the Life of Faith*. Eugene, OR: Cascade, 2020.
Doerr, Anthony. *Four Seasons in Rome: On Twins, Insomnia, and the Biggest Funeral in the History of the World*. New York: Scribner, 2007.
Duffy, Eamon. *Saints and Sinners: A History of the Popes*. New Haven: Yale University Press, 2015.
Egan, Timothy. *A Pilgrimage to Eternity: From Canterbury to Rome in Search of a Faith*. New York: Viking, 2019.
Erasmo, Mario. *Strolling Through Rome: The Definitive Walking Guide to the Eternal City*. London: Tauris Parke, 2015.
Heath, Elizabeth F. *The Architecture Lover's Guide to Rome*. Philadelphia: Pen & Sword, 2019.
Heilbron, J. L. *The Sun in the Church: Cathedrals as Solar Observatories*. Cambridge: Harvard University Press, 1999.
Hughes, Robert. *Rome: A Cultural, Visual, and Personal History*. New York: Vintage, 2011.
Julian of Norwich. *Revelations of Divine Love*. Translated by Clifton Wolters. New York: Penguin, 1966.
Kertzer, David I. *The Kidnapping of Edgardo Mortara*. New York: Vintage, 1998.
Kierkegaard, Søren. *Works of Love*. Edited and translated by Howard V. Hong and Edna H. Hong. Princeton: Princeton University Press, 1995.
Kneale, Matthew. *Rome: A History in Seven Sackings*. New York: Simon & Schuster, 2018.

Bibliography

Loorz, Victoria. *Church of the Wild: How Nature Invites Us into the Sacred.* Minneapolis: Broadleaf, 2021.

Macfarlane, Robert. *The Old Ways: A Journey on Foot.* New York: Penguin, 2012.

Mahoney, Rosemary. *The Singular Pilgrim: Travels on Sacred Ground.* New York: Houghton Mifflin, 2003.

May, Simon. *Love: A History.* New Haven: Yale University Press, 2011.

Merton, Thomas. *The Seven Storey Mountain.* New York: Harcourt Brace Jovanovich, 1948.

Nancy, Jean-Luc. *The Inoperative Community.* Edited by Peter Connor and translated by Christopher Fynsk. Minneapolis: University of Minnesota Press, 1991.

O'Collins, Gerald, and Mario Farrugia. *Catholicism: The Story of Catholic Christianity.* 2nd ed. Oxford: Oxford University Press, 2015.

Parks, Tim. *The Hero's Way: Walking with Garibaldi from Rome to Ravenna.* New York: W. W. Norton, 2021.

Rear, Michael. *Rome: A Pilgrim Guide.* Leominster, UK: Gracewing, 2019.

Rilke, Rainer Maria. *Letters to a Young Poet.* Edited and translated by M.D. Herter Norton. New York: W. W. Norton, 1954.

Rosa, Hartmut. *Resonance: A Sociology of Our Relationship to the World.* Translated by James C. Wagner. Cambridge: Polity, 2019.

Rüpke, Jörg. *Pantheon: A New History of Roman Religion.* Princeton: Princeton University Press, 2018.

Schmisek, Brian. *The Rome of Peter and Paul: A Pilgrim's Guide to New Testament Sites in the Eternal City.* Eugene, OR: Pickwick, 2017.

Shrady, Nicholas. *Sacred Roads: Adventures from the Pilgrimage Trail.* New York: Harper, 1999.

Sloterdijk, Peter. *Spheres, Volume 2: Globes: Macrosphereology.* Translated by Wieland Hoban. South Pasadena, CA: Semiotext(e), 2014.

Sumption, Jonathan. *The Age of Pilgrimage: The Medieval Journey to God.* Mahwah, NJ: HiddenSpring, 2003.

Taylor, Rabun, Katherine Rinne, and Spiro Kostof. *Rome: An Urban History from Antiquity to the Present.* Cambridge: Cambridge University Press, 2016.

Westwood, Jennifer. *On Pilgrimage: Sacred Journeys Around the World.* Mahwah, NJ: HiddenSpring, 2003.

Index

Aquinas, Thomas, 2, 40, 159
Aventine Hill, 1, 3, 40, 193

Basilica del Sacro Cuore di Gesù, 68, 70,
Basilica of Saint Lorenzo in Lucina, 34, 37
Basilica of San Giovanni, 48
Baths of Diocletian, 21, 89
Bruno, Giordano, 89, 94, 109

Campo de' Fiori, 94, 109
Catherine of Siena, Saint, 129, 160
Centrale Montemartini, 42
Chiesa di San Callisto, 10, 13, 17, 22
Chiesa Nuova, 28, 105
Colosseum, 38, 40, 48, 105, 166
Constantine 78, 97, 111, 127, 131, 134, 135, 139, 166, 171
Council of Trent, 106, 107, 159

Heresy, 74, 75, 107, 137

Le Tre Fontane, 77
Luther, Martin, 139, 173, 176, 177

Merton, Thomas, 2, 40
Michelangelo, 11, 29, 30, 89, 159, 182
Miracle, miracles, 26, 28, 58, 82, 118, 183, 194,
Missionaries of the Sacred Heart, 81, 82
Museum of Souls in Purgatory, 81

Orthodoxy, 74, 75, 97, 137, 160, 181,

Pantheon, 95, 157, 161, 162, 164, 165
Pasquino statue, 94, 95
Piazza Navona 22, 26, 94, 95, 97, 105, 111
Porta Flaminia, 13

Sacred Heart of Jesus, 68, 70, 81
Sant'Agnese, 111, 112, 114, 115
Sant'Agostino 22, 72
San Clemente, 48, 49, 50
San Giovanni in Laterano, 48, 131, 134, 138
San Lorenzo fuori le mura, 61, 62
San Nicola Encarcere, 48, 52
San Paolo fuori le Mura, 72, 76, 78
San Pietro, 28, 30, 32, 78, 79, 120, 146, 147, 148, 152, 154, 155, 157, 184,
Sancta Sanctorum, 139, 142
Santa Croce, 106, 170, 171, 173, 174
Santa Maria degli Angeli, 87, 89, 92
Santa Maria della Vittoria 5, 6,
Santa Maria in Aracoeli, 34, 36
Santa Maria in Trastevere, 22, 117
Santa Maria Maggiore, 179, 182, 185
Santa Maria sopra Minerva, 107, 157, 160
Santa Prassede, 117, 119
Santa Sabina on the Aventine Hill, 40
Santi Giovanni e Paulo, 165, 166, 169
Santo Stefano Rotondo, 102, 105, 107
Sistine Chapel, 159, 184, 185
St. Bavo's Cathedral, 122, 124
St. Stephen's Cathedral, 122, 124

Index

Testaccio, 40, 41

Vatican II, 167, 152, 153
Via Appia, 7, 13, 17, 18, 19, 20, 21, 23, 113, 126
Via del Corso, 176

Villa Borghese 34, 129
Villa Medici 87,

XII Apostles Church, 40, 43

Zeno, Saint, 118, 119

www.ingramcontent.com/pod-product-compliance
Lightning Source LLC
Chambersburg PA
CBHW031426150426
43191CB00006B/411